Aiming High

Debra Price

Series Editor: Emma Bartley

GRESHAM BOOKS

© Debra Price 2017

Published by
Gresham Books Limited
The Carriage House
Ningwood Manor
Ningwood
Isle of Wight
PO30 4NJ

Quotes in this publication reflect the views of the individual, not the institution to which they belong.

Main Cover Image: Thinkstock

ISBN 978-0-946095-72-8

Design by Words & Pictures
Typesetting and layout by Fiona Jerome
Printed in the UK

About the Author

Debra Price has taught critical thinking to secondary school students for over ten years, having formerly been Deputy Head and Head of Critical Thinking at Benenden School.

As a passionate advocate of critical thinking, Debra is now working to develop a wide-range of 'critical thinking toolbox' resources to help younger children develop strong thinking skills.

Debra was inspired to write *Aiming High* by parents who asked for their own guide to critical thinking explaining how they could best help their children to become strong critical thinkers.

Today Debra is a director of Gresham Books, a Senior Advisor for RSAcademics and Education Consultant to Harrow International Schools Limited.

Debra is married to Christopher and they live on the Isle of Wight. She is a mother of two and loves to tend her vegetable garden, cook her own produce and travel.

Acknowledgements

This book was inspired by the students that I have been fortunate enough to teach, and the parents who frequently asked me 'Why can't the skills and mind-set of critical thinking be taught to younger children?'
I should like to thank all of my students for showing me how learning to think critically has helped them to reject prejudice, recognise bias, and instead use their own thinking skills to reflect with reason on the world around us.
My ideas and techniques have been influenced by a number of former critical thinking teaching colleagues and I should like to thank them now: Lesley Tyler, Peter Sage, Alfred Nicol and Craig Huxley from whom I learnt so much about how best to open our students' eyes to critical thinking; those who prepared the resources that helped introduce us all to the OCR A Level and AS programmes of Critical Thinking study – Jo Lally, Ruth Matthews, Alison Rowe, Jacqui Thwaites, Colin Hart and Tony McCabe; the work of Professor Guy Claxton, Building Learning Power, has also influenced my interpretation of how best to integrate the skills of critical thinking into a learning environment. I am also grateful to children's newspaper, First News, and its Editor, Nicky Cox MBE for sharing resources; and to Macat and Dr Mike Dash, Chief Research & Development Officer, for their outstanding research on the benefits of critical thinking.
I should like to give special thanks to Emma Bartley for her quiet wisdom and endless patience, and to Nick Oulton for bringing his own indomitable intellect to the project, and to Jane Daubney for her support and encouragement throughout. I am eternally grateful to my children, Isabella and Louis, who have grown up as critical thinkers and for their constant reminders to me to practise what I preach! Lastly, thank you to Christopher, my husband, for his encouragement, care and endless support. I don't say it enough.

Debra Price

Aiming High

CONTENTS

INTRODUCTION

There has never been a more important time to ensure our young people can think critically. In a world where bias, prejudice, self-interest and fanaticism are on the rise, the ability to stand back, evaluate evidence and come to a reasoned conclusion is increasingly necessary. Reason is the method of thinking in an organised, clear way to achieve knowledge and understanding. This use of reason is one of the very qualities that makes us human, and the application of reason is at the heart of all human endeavour that has brought about progress.

We can all cite situations, both in our personal and professional lives as well as in world events, where the failure to think critically and apply reason has led to conflict, and poor decision making. In the worst scenarios, it can lead to hurtful actions, criminal activity or even genocide.

No one would say that reason is more important than emotion. Enjoying and celebrating our emotions is a central part of human nature. However, making decisions simply from an emotional basis can be indulgent and misguided: being able to apply a methodology of logic and reason to instinctive feelings or thoughts, can often temper difficulties, solve problems, and bring harmony and order. This is as true within family life as it is within politics. Learning a few simple rules of how to think critically is quick to do, and even the youngest children can begin to do this.

Research from child psychology has shown that even very young children possess at least the rudimentary ability to create what, in critical thinking language, is called 'an argument — the ability to support a conclusion with a reason, and then with evidence. Children are able to reap the benefits of reasoning from a very young age. Often parents will reason with their children sub-consciously—'If you eat your vegetables, you will grow strong and healthy'—a perfect example of hypothetical reasoning! However, as soon as children start to argue in this way, bias can emerge and children can be victims of the same prejudices that affect adults when they use reasoning in the wrong way. Teaching children to recognise bias and to attempt to become clear, objective thinkers, can be the domain of sensible, responsible parenting just as much as it can be taught in schools.

Learning to think rationally involves becoming more open-minded about what is true, and requires the ability to change one's mind. It involves moving away from the position of 'because I said so' and to the position where an idea is treated on its own merits when held up for examination. It involves scrutinising what we are told and deciding whether we should believe it or not. Essentially, it is about growing up. Adding to the CT repertoire as a child grows, and teaching strategies appropriate to the child's age, gives a young person an armoury of intellectual tools to battle their way through the complexities of childhood and adolescence.

This book gives parents a structured, sensible way to apply the principles of critical thinking within their family context. Using simple mnemonics to remember a method to evaluate evidence or judge credibility (eg RAVEN) can be used by children as young as eight or nine and will last a lifetime. Being able to recognise the flaws in the arguments or opinions of others ensures young teenagers will not be hoodwinked and taken advantage of.

There are academic advantages too, to being able to think and write in a structured and organised way. Children who can apply some basic critical thinking principles are likely to do better at school, in entrance exams and in public examinations. They will be more confident and articulate speakers and will always have a method they can use when being confronted with unseen material. The beauty of learning the language of critical thinking is that it is completely transferable across all academic subjects, and research shows that students who learn the vocabulary and methods of critical thinking, do better in exams than those who do not.

As an adult who came to the methodology of critical thinking as a teacher, it has transformed the way I approach complex decision making and view current affairs. I wish I had had the toolkit when I was a parent of young children, as I expect my family life would have been more harmonious! I thoroughly recommend this book to you, and hope you will reap the benefits for many years to come.

Lesley Tyler,
Deputy Head Academic
Benenden School

WHAT IS CRITICAL THINKING?

Learning is the result of thinking. We all think, but much of our thinking tends to be reactive, can often be uninformed, and may well be distorted by prejudices that we don't even realise we have. Helping your child to think critically gives your child the ability to think clearly and rationally about what to believe, say, write and do. Not surprisingly 'better thinking' results in 'better learning'.

Critical thinking, or CT, is all about processes. It is about developing good thinking habits that are fully transferable across all of your child's subjects, as well as into daily life. The tools that we will make available in this book will help your child take problems and challenges in their stride and ultimately relish the opportunity to provide their own creative solutions.

Being top of the class, achieving A*s or winning a place at a top university all depend on your child's ability to demonstrate higher order critical thinking skills. The good news is that these skills *can* be taught, encouraged and nurtured by parents and reinforced at home, or indeed in virtually any setting. Using the processes of CT can help your child to:
▶

IN THE KNOW

'Being an accomplished critical thinker requires an open, yet critical, approach to one's own thinking as well as that of others.'

Beth Black, Senior Research Officer, Cambridge Assessment

MONKEY BUSINESS IMAGES LTD/THINKSTOCK

- Improve intelligence (intelligence is *not* fixed) and maximise learning potential
- Excel as a learner in the classroom
- Improve exam performance including at 11+, scholarship, GCSE and A Level
- Excel in interviews
- Develop thinking, questioning and resolution skills for daily living
- Demonstrate the skills that 21st century employers are looking for
- Become a good citizen and make judgements about moral, ethical and social issues

So what is critical thinking? CT focuses on a series of processes that help your child to develop the higher order thinking skills of:

- ANALYSIS
- EVALUATION
- SYNTHESIS
- SELF REFLECTION
- SELF CORRECTION

A critical thinker is able to:
- Analyse arguments
- Judge for themselves the relevance and significance of information
- Evaluate claims and their sources
- Navigate dilemmas and difficult choices
- Form well-reasoned judgements and decisions

Bad thinking habits lead to sloppy thinking and sloppy thinking leads to sloppy learning. So ideally the basics of critical thinking should be introduced

as early as possible. Teachers and your child's school environment will obviously begin this process, but there is a great deal you can do to support and accelerate your child's efforts to build strong critical thinking foundations.

Active, careful thinking leads to powerful learning which in turn leads to academic success. As a parent you can set the scene to help develop good thinking habits very early. The earlier your child learns to avoid the pitfalls of reactive, uninformed or prejudiced thinking the more likely they are to maximise their own learning potential. Mastering CT skills means 'learning to learn', and once your child does this, their progress as an effective learner will become turbocharged. ∎

HOW CAN I HELP MY CHILD DEVELOP CRITICAL THINKING SKILLS?

The great news is that developing your child's critical thinking skills is simple: you don't need to drag them round museums and cathedrals (although these will provide some great learning opportunities too), or buy sophisticated 'educational' toys. Opportunities to learn come in all shapes and sizes—and with a little parental wisdom, all sorts of daily tasks around the home, from laying the table to wrapping presents, can become a learning experience.

Problem solving

If your child believes you see them as a problem solver, they are far more likely to see themselves in this way. The reverse is equally true: if your child believes you think they can't do something, this can affect their readiness to have a go.

▶

WHAT'S HOLDING THEM BACK?

Children (and adults) need to be in the right frame of mind for successful problem solving. Even something that you might consider relatively trivial could affect your child's concentration or shake their confidence. If your child's attitude to learning has altered, try to find out what might be the cause.

Achieving the right balance is tricky. On the one hand, it isn't practical to live life at the pace necessary to let your child do everything by themselves. Yes, your five–year–old could choose, weigh, bag up and load into the trolley each of the five-a-day fruit and vegetables you are buying in the supermarket, but you may not always have time for that.

On the other hand, the more you do for your child, the less they are learning to do for themselves and the harder it becomes for them to believe in their own problem-solving abilities. And there comes a point when you will have to factor do-it-yourself shoelace tying into the morning routine.

As with most things, a balanced approach is probably best. By giving your child problems to solve, you will encourage them to think and behave as a problem solver. A 'problem' can be any task that you are happy to delegate to them, and that you are willing to let them find their own way of doing (with a little—but not too much—guidance). The first time you give the task to your child, the results are likely to be far from perfect, but by allowing trial and error to take place, two great things will happen: the job will get done better, and your child's powers of evaluation will get stronger too. And, best of all, if your child sees that you believe in their problem-solving abilities—then so will they.

Although we all lead busy lives, there are many points in the day where you can introduce some thinking opportunities—during the school run, or at meal times perhaps. Introducing a 'thinking' question or idea should be fun, not a tedious chore, and it need only take a few minutes. Aim for quality not quantity of thinking time; you are simply hoping to excite your child's interest and help start the process of exploration and active thinking.

Asking questions

Posing a thought-provoking question is an important part of helping your child to learn to become a good critical thinker. Questions have the capacity to help improve your child's understanding and make sense of the world around them. Asking questions, and speculating about possible answers, also reinforces the basic idea that learning is a journey, and often there is no right or wrong answer. One of the biggest potential obstacles to your child's potential as a critical thinker is a fear of getting things wrong. Asking your child lots of challenging questions, and helping them work through their thinking, will help them get over their worries about not knowing the answer.

Arguably, virtually all of the world's great breakthroughs happened when an individual responded to a question with a creative answer. Think of the steam engine, the Internet, or innumerable medical advances.

The best kind of questions are those that help kickstart your child's critical and creative thinking skills by encouraging them to develop, justify or even review and reform their ideas.

As a parent, you and your child will share a great many sights, sounds and events in daily life and these small daily occurrences provide ample opportunity for you to ask questions to excite your child's interest in the world around them.

Peer pressure

Peer pressure can intimidate your child and prevent them from taking enough thinking time. Picture the scene in a classroom when hands shoot up in instant response to a teacher's question. This scenario may soon be a thing of the past as 'thinking time' and 'hands down' are becoming recognised classroom techniques to encourage

'When your child calls down the stairs for the fifth time that week complaining that they don't have the right clothes, you start to wonder why they can't do anything for themselves. That's because they have sussed you out: they know that you find it easier just to do the job for them. (There are more irritating things in life than watching a teenager reluctantly "help" put on a load of laundry—but not many.) To change things, we found that we had to turn the lack of clean pants into our child's problem. Then, the job would get done. Pants would be found. By doing this at home, although it was certainly more than a one-off inconvenience, we helped them to stand on their own two feet.'

JONATHAN WILSON, PARENT AND ASSISTANT HEAD

METABATA FLOW / THINKSTOCK

IN THE KNOW

'Critical thinking is about asking questions—the right questions. It's about not accepting things on trust. It's about empathy, not least having the self-awareness to accept that you may get things wrong. And it's about finding new and creative solutions where others see only problems.'

Dr Mike Dash, Chief Research & Development Officer, Macat, November 2015

children to reflect and think before they answer a question.

In a test situation most children worry when 'everybody else seems to be writing but me'. You can reassure your child that often the person who starts writing last is the person who has truly thought through the question and therefore gets the best mark. Advise your child to focus only on their own efforts, not on those around them, and to go at their own speed. Make it clear that worrying about what other people are doing is not going to help them achieve their best.

Using technology

Electronic technology provides some amazing possibilities for learning—but e-devices can also distract and interrupt your child's concentration. Technology encourages instant responses—which is very much at odds with the need to think about, persevere and work through a problem. It is important to encourage your child to take the time to work something out, without becoming dependent on the technology that would make it easy—no simple task!

▶

5 TYPES OF **QUESTIONS** TO ASK YOUR CHILD

1 Questions that build on information such as a sight, sound or event.
• Has this happened before?
• What might have caused that?

2 Questions that ask why problems are arising, or why patterns are developing.
• Why do you think this happened?
• Why do you suppose squirrels like it best in that tree?
• Why did you decide that was the right answer?

3 Questions that get your child to think creatively by speculating about what they don't know.
• What might happen if we…?
• Which do you think is the best way?
• If there were no alphabet, how would you communicate on paper?

4 Questions that encourage empathy (see page 18) will reinforce the need to consider issues from more than one point of view.
• How does this affect you?
• How does it affect other people?
• Would you make the same decision if you had known how your friends felt?

5 Questions that encourage your child to use their knowledge and understanding to answer questions and offer solutions.
• How would you teach Grandma to use an iPhone?
• What is the fairest way of deciding which film to watch?
• How shall we decide which charities we should support this year?

Set the right conditions

It's easy to forget just how much children can be affected by low blood sugar or lack of sleep. Hungry, tired children are not likely to be in the mood to problem solve or learn well (or, indeed, learn at all!). Try to ensure that your child has a good routine and gets the sleep they need (9–11 hours is recommended for 6 to 11-year-olds).

A healthy, balanced diet is necessary for your child to make the most of their own natural thinking ability. Be aware of the impact of sugar highs which can create unhelpful peaks and troughs in your child's ability to concentrate. ∎

MOODBOARD/THINKSTOCK

THE IMPORTANCE
OF MAKING MISTAKES

Many of mankind's greatest discoveries started life as mistakes: penicillin, X-rays and microwave ovens to name a few. But no matter how often you hear that the very best learning can arise from getting something wrong, making a mistake still feels uncomfortable. Children naturally seek approval both from adults and their peers, and when approval is firmly tied to getting the answer right, playing it safe soon becomes preferable to having a go. The best critical thinkers are curious, ready to explore and experiment, happy to see what works and

unafraid to discover what doesn't. Fortunately, this spirit of curiosity is innate in children; all it needs is to be nurtured.

Learning courage

Learning courage is what enables children to see a mistake not as a failure but as an opportunity. Stepping outside the binary mindset of 'right' or 'wrong' frees children to try out questions like, 'What happens if I do it this way?' The answers to these questions will help your child learn and improve each time.

When your child has confidence in their natural skills of **analysis** and **evaluation**, they will be able to reflect on what they know and will be ready to try and make sense of a new challenge. But key to this is learning to accept that it is not only alright to get things wrong; it is positively helpful.

A parent's role

Parents play a vital role in helping their child develop the **resilience** that leads to learning courage. In addition, learning how to learn from mistakes develops other valuable skills such as **resourcefulness**, **perseverance** and **determination**—all excellent qualities for successful lifelong learning.

Children learn out of necessity. Think about your child's first messy attempts to use a spoon, or perhaps learn to stand. If you had intervened by feeding your child because they were trying to use the spoon upside down, or by giving a helping hand whenever they wanted to stand, there would have been no reason for them to learn how to handle the situation themselves.

Most important of all is celebrating and encouraging a child's search for the best solution, rather than the solution itself. Fear of getting something wrong is arguably the greatest potential block to learning at every level of education.

'I remember my son building a tower out of wooden blocks, slowly developing an awareness of how many blocks were needed to make the tower (remembering and understanding), and then applying his understanding to begin construction. Gradually analysis took place as he realised that a tower built one brick on another was likely to fall over very easily—but was likely to make the tallest tower. A bigger base and a shorter tower was likely to be the safer but much less exciting option. Finally, my son built the tower his way—a hybrid of safe but tall! But what if I, or my husband, had always built the tower for our son? Aside from it being far less fun for him, no learning would have taken place and he would not have had the chance to begin the process of developing his skills as a critical thinker.'

DEBRA PRICE

MARK BOWDEN/THINKSTOCK

USE THIS AT SCHOOL

'One of the recurring themes in my conversations with the pupils, be they in small groups, individually or in assembly, is that I want them to be bold. I advise them repeatedly: take chances and accept any failures as a powerful learning experience but always remember, I tell them, the greatest failure of all is not to have tried. Teachers need to provide risk-taking opportunities and to embrace mistakes as a vital part of the learning process. By minimising the pain of getting it wrong, they increase the pupils' confidence levels and encourage them to have a go—even when they are not sure they are right.'

– Debbie Leonard, Headmistress

Research indicates that intelligence—or IQ—is not fixed at birth; parents and educators can intervene to help the learning process. The most important thing a parent can do to maximise their child's IQ is to create a home environment that nurtures the 'have a go spirit' and applauds and celebrates a child's pursuit of 'trial and error'. This environment will help them progress through the learning stages to develop their own powers of evaluation and creativity.

It is never too early to do all you can to create a home environment that recognises mistakes as essential stepping stones to powerful learning.

Your child's attitude to learning is shaped by your reactions to their efforts. Children are excellent observers of their parents and are highly attuned to praise or disapproval in voice or facial expressions. Understandably, children want praise and they will adapt their actions accordingly to get it. A reaction like, 'Oh no, that's wrong' discourages your child from working out a problem for themselves.

So, praise your child's efforts—and make clear your praise is for their effort, determination, resilience and resourcefulness, not for the outcome. ■

WORKING TOGETHER WITH MY CHILD'S SCHOOL

NICHOLAS DALE/THINKSTOCK

Good teamwork between parent and teacher will ensure your child makes the best possible progress in developing active critical thinking skills.

Your child's time at school will, of course, be extremely important in helping them become a strong critical thinker. However, given that so many hours will be spent at home, your influence and support are powerful factors in them achieving success. Supporting your child's teacher means working in the same direction, using similar techniques and not accidentally thwarting a teacher's game plan.

Make sure you understand the teaching techniques used at your child's school. Like you, teachers will be trying to build your child's intellectual confidence, to encourage them to give things a go, and to instil in them a love of exploration and learning—and so you can work together to continue this mission outside the classroom. Ask your child's teachers for advice about learning opportunities in the home environment.

Don't give too much help

Think long term: when your child is given a project or a creative task, most of the benefit will be in your child learning about trial and error. Teachers want your child to do the task themselves—so that they can start thinking. This means letting your child experiment with what works and what doesn't; giving too much help will deny your child the journey of learning. So, don't be tempted to try and shortcut the learning and experimenting process (and definitely don't be tempted to do your child's

homework for them!); the end result matters far less than how your child got there. You can best support the teacher by trying to be in tune with the learning process rather than focusing too much on the end result.

Prepare your child to learn

A key part of learning to be an effective critical thinker is knowing when you

USE THIS AT SCHOOL

'I want children in my class to experiment and to work things out for themselves.'

– Year 1 Teacher

USE THIS AT SCHOOL

'I understand that all parents want their child to come 'top of the class'—but giving their child the answers now will actually hamper a child's ability to learn to be self-sufficient and work things out for themselves. Parents won't be able to be with their child in a test situation!'

– Year 2 Teacher

need to know more and realising that you have the power to fill in some of the knowledge gaps yourself. So, if your child is doing a project on dinosaurs, encourage them not to leave all of the work to their teacher, but to do some independent fact finding for themselves. Even just looking up some key dinosaur words or studying pictures will give your child the opportunity to become more resourceful and independent in their learning. Having practised using these critical thinking skills at home, your child will be better prepared to use them at school.

'I recently had dinner out with some friends, together with our two sons, aged eight and four. As our conversation drifted onto rather uninteresting adult matters, my eight-year-old immersed himself in a small experiment at the table, trying to work out whether salt or sugar dissolved faster with an ice cube or a few teaspoons of water. My son told our friends that he had carried out this experiment in every restaurant or café we had visited recently and was close to declaring his findings! Although my four-year-old didn't join in the measuring and dissolving, he was certainly very much enjoying being a part of the "spirit of exploration".'
MOTHER OF TWO

Encourage resilience and self-reliance

When your child asks for help, get in the habit of checking that they have first had a 'proper' go at resolving the problem, and taken some steps to find out for themselves what to do. Questions like, 'So what have you done so far?' or 'What do you think you should try next?' will help encourage this. ■

©GAM/THINKSTOCK

EMPATHY

mpathy involves considering and respecting the opinions of others. An effective critical thinker keeps an open mind and is prepared to look, listen and reflect on a range of factors before judging a situation.

However, keeping a genuinely open mind can be very hard because most of us are influenced by what we already know (or think we know), not to mention what we are told or what we hear or read. All of these sources of information will help us form a point of view but they only provide a small piece of the jigsaw, almost certainly not enough to get a genuine understanding of the whole picture.

Empathy necessitates imagining what a situation feels like for other people and as such is a vital part of critical thinking. However, the natural inclination of many children, well into young adulthood, is to see the world only as it relates to them. Learning to develop empathy will help your child consider other people's feelings and reactions, especially when these involve views that your child instinctively doesn't agree with. Empathetic skills will enable your child to gain a 360 degree perspective on a problem or situation.

Far more importantly, empathy forms the basis of good behaviour and will help prevent bad behaviour such as rudeness, or worse still bullying. Being able to empathise will help your child relate to individuals and understand that other people's happiness is as important as their own.

Children's first and most important experience of empathy is the love and attention shown to them by their parents. Children are also acutely tuned in to observing the empathy—or lack of it—that adults around them show other people. If a parent ignores the waitress who serves them coffee, their child will notice. Similarly, children will notice adults valuing and empathising with one another.

Empathy is a skill that can be taught and that improves with regular practice. The child who learns to consider how others are feeling is

DIGITAL VISION/THINKSTOCK

> **Do you have both sides of the story? Encourage your child to get both sides of the story before they make up their own mind.**

developing a really great life skill, one that will naturally lead them to be an open-minded and reflective thinker.

Note to child: It's not all about you!
An important developmental milestone is when a young child begins to understand that their parents exist independently of them. This realisation is often helped along by siblings who play a vital role in dispelling any misapprehension about who is the centre of the universe. A child who thinks the world revolves around them (because that's how they are treated) will find it very hard to empathise with others and consider different points of view.

Manners maketh empathy
Getting children to write their thank

you letters after Christmas and birthdays can be a thankless task (ironically), but it's one of the best ways to ensure thinking about the feelings of other people becomes a habit. Explain that thank you cards, texts or emails will always be warmly received and demonstrate that the sender has thought about and noticed what has been done for them.

Accentuate the positive
Your child needs your guidance to develop their empathetic skills. Sometimes more weight is given to correcting a child's negative behaviour, say, if they snatch a toy from a sibling. Take care to give just as much attention to praising positive empathetic actions such as sharing, and thinking of others first. ■

9 WAYS TO **ENCOURAGE EMPATHY**

1 Friendships. If—or when—your child falls out with a friend, encourage them to think about how their friend is feeling. If your child has upset someone by something they have said, ask them to think how they would feel if someone said the same thing to them.

2 Another point of view. When your child reads a story, ask them how they think each character was feeling and why they acted as they did—especially the villain character.

3 Good manners. Whether it's saying please and thank you, not being too noisy on a train or bus, or not pushing in ahead of other people in a queue, explain to your child that good manners are all about considering the feelings and situations of others. Ask your child how they feel when people don't treat them with good manners and encourage them to understand that good manners should be applied to everyone.

4 Everyone matters. Understanding that everyone matters is essential if your child is going to grow up to respect and reflect on the views of others.

5 Challenge prejudices. When your child tells you they do or don't like something (or someone), ask them how they came to that conclusion. Was it because they really tried to get to know the person, or found out the facts about the thing? Or was it a knee-jerk reaction based on appearance or first impressions? Illustrate the point with a 'blindfold' tasting test of some foods that your child might have said they aren't keen on. When your child can't see what they are eating, the results are likely to surprise you both.

6 Need to know. Keeping an open mind is an invaluable life skill and part of this skill is recognising that you often don't know enough to make an informed opinion, particularly in cases where only one side of the story, or point of view, has been put forward. Try and make finding out as much as possible an important part of your child's decision-making process.

7 Differences. Empathising with other people comes more easily if they look and seem like us; it's much more of a challenge when all we notice are differences. Discuss different cultures with your child. A good start might be asking your child what they know about the different cultures of classmates or other children at school.

8 Stop and think. By now your child should know that you expect them to be able to pause and consider more than one point of view. Explain that while they don't have to agree with an opposing view, they should certainly try to understand it. The next time you and your child disagree about something, ask them to consider your concerns and why you think as you do. Similarly, show that you are doing exactly the same thing when you try to consider your child's viewpoint.

9 Help yourself. A key part of learning to become a strong critical thinker means being prepared to find out more and inform yourself. This needs resilience and tenacity. The next time your child says, 'The teacher didn't explain it very well and wouldn't help me' ask your child what they have done to help themselves. Have they tried to work through the problem? Have they consulted notes, or a text book, or perhaps asked someone else in the class? Encourage your child to become their own best learning resource.

SHIRONOSOV/THINKSTOCK

CRITICAL THINKING PRACTICE

BALUZEK/THINKSTOCK

In this book we give some suggestions for activities that allow your child to put their critical thinking skills to the test. Very young children (5–7) learn by trying to make sense of what is going on around them. Think of how a child acquires simple skills—such as how to build structures with blocks or Lego. By trial and error they learn which pieces to connect, or what might make the structure fall

over. They will test what they have learnt, driven forward by the ambition to build the structure bigger or better. This is active learning.

Older children (7–11) naturally want to try things out for themselves. By taking a step back you help them become 'problem solvers'. Encourage them to analyse what is going on, evaluate what works best and come up with their own theories of what would

work even better.

Once they get to about 11, your child's school work is likely to include preparing for important tests. It can be hard, but try to resist the temptation to encourage them to cram knowledge for the sake of boosting marks. Deep and lasting learning is far more likely to come when your child understands for themselves where they are going wrong. ■

Activities for the very young (5–7 years)

BLOCKS AND PLAYDOUGH

All kinds of practical 'hands on' play such as building structures with blocks or making patterns in playdough will help develop your child's critical thinking skills. You can help by incorporating a 'What happens next?' moment: 'What happens when the blocks are built on an angle?' Or, 'How thin does the playdough have to be before it breaks?' Allowing your child's play experiments to fail (safely!) is important because it leads to the all-important stage: evaluation. Let your child analyse and work with the resources at their disposal, then evaluate the problems, and then try out a solution. If something isn't working, encourage your child to try a different approach: Why did the tower fall over? Will it always fall? How could the tower be built differently?

JACKF/THINKSTOCK

DEN BUILDING

Activities such as den building (indoors or outdoors), where the child must source and evaluate the materials, are huge fun and great opportunities for problem solving and resourcefulness. If your child enjoys painting, let them mix their own paints. What happens when the paint is too runny or too thick? How can they get the consistency that works for them?

WRAPPING PRESENTS

They will need to consider shapes and areas as they work out how much paper each gift requires. They will also be delighted that you trust them with such a precious task.

SIMPLE COOKING

This activity can be made age appropriate—and it's a skill for life. At this age a simple recipe like making chocolate cornflake cakes is great for experimenting with consistencies and volumes. Cooking simple recipes will give your child some great 'what happens next?' moments (under your supervision).

• Scrambling eggs—what makes the eggs go hard?
• Whipping cream—how much whipping makes the cream go stiff?
• Mashing potatoes—what makes mashed potatoes go creamy?

OTHER ACTIVITIES TO TRY

• Lay the table
• Design a birthday card
• Make a snowball/snowman
• Build a sandcastle
• Sing a song
• Recite a poem
• Mix paints
• Build a matchstick house
• Wade into a puddle (with wellies on!)
• Make a musical instrument

Activities for 7–11 years

Children of this age naturally want to try things out for themselves. By taking a step back you help them become 'problem solvers'. Encourage them to analyse what is going on, evaluate what works best and come up with their own theories of what might work even better. Resist the temptation to do the analysis and evaluation for your child, whether this is in creative play, or with a piece of school work. The most powerful learning happens when they start to evaluate concepts for themselves. When your child hits a problem you can help them by asking open-ended questions such as, 'Interesting idea—what would happen if you did it a bit differently?' Or, 'How about changing that bit?' This will affirm and endorse your child's efforts and cast them in the role of a '**problem solver**'. This approach encourages your child to treat a mistake or a problem as just an opportunity to analyse, evaluate and come up with their own creative solution.

COOKERY
Why did the cake collapse? What recipe makes the best chocolate brownie? Was it because there was more butter or chocolate? Why won't the scone dough stick together—does it need more flour or water? Bake a tray of scones—what happens if the dough is too runny or too dry?

INDOOR/OUTDOOR GARDENING
Why did the plant grow/why did it die? Did the plant need more sunlight or water?

DOG TRAINING
What techniques are most successful in training a puppy—praise or a tit-bit to endorse good behaviour?

PACKING
Encourage your child to pack their own school bag the night before school (rather than leave it to you to remember what you think they will forget). If they forget something—they will learn from having done so.

SHOPPING
On a trip to the supermarket, give them part of your shopping list—say, vegetables to choose and weigh. When each task is done, always encourage your child to tell you what they are pleased with and what didn't work so well, and what they would do differently next time.

MEAL PLANNING
Ask your child to help plan family meals, working around a few ground rules set by you. These could be that the meal needs to have some fruit or vegetables, or be someone's favourite, or not too expensive. Get your child to make a chart with meals and highlight them with different stickers to show if the meal is particularly healthy, someone's favourite, good value, or perhaps is a really naughty but very nice occasional treat! Ideally, your child should be aiming for a chart that has a good cross-section of stickers.

OTHER ACTIVITIES TO TRY
• Make a dam in a stream
• Make a birthday video message
• Draw a self portrait
• Learn how to do a handstand or cartwheel
• Do the washing up
• Learn how to eat with chop-sticks
• Make a water-proof den
• Learn how to fly a kite

MONKEY BUSINESS IMAGES LTD/THINKSTOCK

Activities for 11–13 years

At this age your child's school work is likely to include preparing for important tests. It can be hard, but try to resist the temptation to encourage them to cram—or spoon-feed—knowledge for the sake of boosting marks. Deep and lasting learning is far more likely to come when your child understands for themselves where they are going wrong. If your child makes a mistake, praise their attempts to find out what went wrong. Keep encouraging your child to adopt a problem-solving mindset. Always make clear it is the 'have-a-go' spirit that will win your praise, not a perfect outcome. Don't give help until your child has first taken steps to help themselves. This means expecting your child to persevere and check information for themselves first.

CURRENT AFFAIRS
Discuss current affairs stories with your child. If they don't know enough about the event to have a discussion, encourage them to find out more themselves from newspapers or news websites. Tell them that you would like to know more about the story and ask them to explain both points of view to you.

JOURNEY PLANNING
Give your child the task of route planning for a long walk—or researching travel options for a family holiday, matching them against family members' likes and dislikes.

CATERING
Entrust your child with the shopping and catering for a special occasion when their effort, tenacity and problem-solving skills can be admired by the whole family.

OTHER ACTIVITIES TO TRY
- Draw a self portrait
- Plan a bedroom or work space
- Cryptic crosswords or sudoku
- Follow instructions to assemble a model
- Photograph the world around them
- Teach a younger sibling how to do up their shoelaces or lay the table
- Work out the quickest route

COOKERY—WHAT WORKS AND WHAT DOESN'T
- Make some pasta dough—it's only flour and eggs; knead it, and roll it out and cut it into sheets or shapes
- Teach another family member how to make something new

© SERGIO KUMER/THINKSTOCK

WAVEBREAKMEDIA LTD/THINKSTOCK

WHY SHOULD I LEARN
CRITICAL
THINKING TOO?

Parents are a child's most important role model and the way in which they handle the big and small issues of daily life is arguably the greatest influence on their child's behaviour. The processes of critical thinking provide a step-by-step guide to how to think clearly and rationally through any situation.

Why should I learn critical thinking too?

If you want your child to become an effective critical thinker they will need to see you demonstrate 'critical thinking in action'. This means supporting your point of view with reasons and evidence, admitting when you don't know the facts and need

to find out more, working out what sources you can trust, being prepared to consider other points of view, or being able to spot when others are trying to manipulate you with fear or prejudice.

Similarly, if you want your child to be a problem solver, wherever possible they need to see this attitude modelled in the 'grown-up' world. Talk to your child about mistakes you have made and explain what you learnt and what you might do differently. Don't be afraid to say, 'I got that wrong. Next time I will...'

Thinking critically means being aware that we are constantly learning and being informed by the world around us. As a parent there is no-one

better placed to guide your child on this journey. ∎

'Parenting is hard work and some days are better than others. We are not perfect, and we all have bad moments (or days, or weeks!). It's hard to be on display all day every day, but the truth is that our kids are watching. They look to us for clues on how to interact with others, how to solve problems, how to resolve conflict, how to make friends and how to cope with big emotions.'
MICHELE OBAMA

WORKING OUT MEANING

The ability to extract meaning and communicate thoughts and ideas effectively will play a very important part in helping your child do well in lessons, exams and interviews. This is why developing analytical and comprehension skills plays such a significant part in the National Curriculum in England at Key Stages 1 and 2.

The student who can cut to the heart of the matter and isolate and define key ideas and concepts is using higher order thinking skills that are necessary to ace any test—from an end of year quiz to an Oxbridge interview.

Understanding and employing critical thinking habits will help your child extract meaning. In particular, you should be helping them to activate their senses and learn to pay attention to the information that their senses are providing; this means developing active looking, hearing, tasting, smelling and touching skills.

Encouraging your child to learn to take 'thinking time' is an important part of helping them pay attention to the information provided by their senses.

Active looking is a precursor to active reading, and should be encouraged in children of all ages. ■

THE GREAT 'SWITCH-ON'

How many of us have messed up an exam because we didn't read the question properly, or answered the wrong number of questions? Or perhaps we signed something without reading the small print? Learning to see and notice is an invaluable skill, and learning it early teaches our brains to pay attention. It is far easier to glance, skim-read, or just have a general look at something. Getting into the habit of noticing the all important little details, and taking time to consider what they mean, can be hard work.

Learning to be aware, 'switch on' and make the very most of senses, or abilities, that we already have is at the heart of critical thinking. Your child already has the ability to find and retrieve information, they just need to switch on their 'active looking' skills to help them do so. Encouraging your child to be observant, notice the little things, and pay close attention to detail will help them work out what is important and construct meaning.

At Key Stage 2 many children find it challenging to notice enough; this may be because they are tempted to respond to the first thing they see on the page rather than systematically look at the whole page, and then take time to reflect. You can help your child develop 'active looking' skills by encouraging them to look, see and then think about what they are seeing. Later, this will help them master the demands of English at Key Stages 1 and 2.

Thinking time

Taking just five or ten seconds to think over an answer is likely to produce a far better response than a first reaction. When you ask your child a question, encourage them to spend longer thinking and reflecting before they answer. Taking just 10 to 15 seconds longer to reflect will almost certainly generate a more thoughtful and insightful answer. Encouraging your child to use thinking time to improve their answers is a critical thinking habit that will bring almost immediate benefits to your child's learning. ■

USE THIS AT SCHOOL

The habits of critical thinking can be tremendously powerful in helping your child master the demands of English at Key Stages 1 and 2. At these levels there is great emphasis on isolating and retrieving meaning from words, understanding the significance of information, and considering how pictures or symbols might add valuable information. Before they apply this to their reading, they should be encouraged to develop the powers of active looking.

SIMONKR/THINKSTOCK

CRITICAL THINKING PRACTICE

In this book we give some suggestions for activities that allow your child to put their critical thinking skills to the test. Very young children (5–7) learn by trying to make sense of what is going on around them. Think of how a child acquires simple skills—such as how to build structures with blocks or Lego. By trial and error they learn which pieces to connect, or what might make the structure fall over. They will test what they have learnt, driven forward by the ambition to build the structure bigger or better. This is active learning.

Older children (7–11) naturally want to try things out for themselves. By taking a step back you help them become 'problem solvers'. Encourage them to analyse what is going on, evaluate what works best and come up with their own theories of what would work even better. ▶

5–7 years 'Sensory switch-on' activities

1. On a walk in a park or the country, ask your child to describe what they see, smell, hear and touch. How many legs does an insect have? How many different shaped leaves can they find, or how many different colours of brown or green?

2. At home, pick out two different fruits or vegetables and ask your child to observe what is the same about them (shape/texture/colour etc), and what is different.

3. Play simple number or symbol recognition games, such as easy card games, that help your child become adept at looking and seeing.

4. Go stargazing and paint a starry night.

5. Draw your happy face.

6. Play I-spy.

7. Play miming games.

8. How many different fruits and vegetables can they find in the supermarket.

9. On a car journey, make a list of the different cars they see.

10. Taste test: work out how much juice to mix with water to make it taste right. How would they describe the different tastes of a slice of orange, lemon or lime?

8–11 years 'Sensory switch-on' activities

1. Encourage your child to practise 'active looking' skills to notice key details in everyday situations. For example, when driving down a street, ask them to count the lamp posts, or letter boxes, or bicycles.

2. What messages do these symbols or pictures communicate? Ask your child to explain their thinking: what do they think these clues mean? Could there be any other meanings?

3. Draw a map from home to school.

4. Make a treasure map and go on a treasure hunt.

5. Follow a wildlife trail (footprints). What do the different footprints tell them about the bird or animal?

6. Pick some fresh fruit—what are the signs that the fruit is ripe and juicy?

7. Play charades.

8. Taste test: decide whether something needs more salt or sugar.

9. Smell test: see how many fruits they can identify by smell alone.

WOEVALE/THINKSTOCK

11–13 years 'Sensory switch-on' activities

1. Do a really difficult jigsaw puzzle.

2. Try some difficult 'spot the difference' puzzles.

3. Study a photograph of a cathedral or castle, and then try to draw it from memory.

4. Go stargazing and draw a constellation.

5. Study a map and then try to describe what sort of terrain it depicts.

6. Look at pictures of famous paintings or sculptures. Describe what you do and do not like about these works of art.

7. Taste test: decide whether something is sweet or sour, or needs more herbs or spices.

8. Touch test: see how many materials (woods/plastics/metals) can be identified by touch alone.

TIPS FOR PARENTS

Strong critical thinking depends on gathering as much information as possible about a situation before trying to evaluate it. Getting used to actively using your senses provides a great way to help inform day-to-day living. Show your child how you 'switch on' and use your senses to gather more information about the world around you, and how much you depend on your senses in daily life. Smell and taste are invaluable guides to helping identify fresh ingredients or well-cooked food. Often we can work out how someone is feeling by the way they look or sound.

Explain how Braille provides blind people with a system of reading and writing by using their sense of touch, or how deaf people communicate by using their sight to decode sign language. ■

HEMERA/GETTY/THINKSTOCK

ACTIVE READING

Accomplished critical thinkers must learn how to gather information, before they can evaluate it. Learning to become an 'active reader' is a key part of this, and builds on the skills of getting used to using all of your senses, especially 'active looking'.

Active reading means reading with a clear purpose. Reading pages about a topic from a textbook in the hope that knowledge will somehow 'sink in' is a passive technique which is likely to have limited benefits.

Knowledge is formed, and understanding created, when you see and make connections between ideas and facts. To help this process along it is necessary to ask questions of reading, try to see patterns emerging, and seek out links between concepts.

Active reading is a bit like going fishing; you have to set out to try and 'catch' something from the reading with a kind of 'learning net'. Before you start reading you need to throw your net across the reading so that, as you read, you catch important points and facts; then you can inspect your 'learning catch' and see what you make of it.

For example, if your child was studying for a science test, and wanted to learn about how animals and plants adapt to their environment, they might read a general chapter about animals and plants in the desert. However, rather than just reading the whole chapter, an active reader would pose themselves a series of learning questions before they even started to read. Typically, these questions might strive to achieve an overview, perhaps by trying to identify the 5Ws: who, what, why, when and where. Searching for the 5Ws would lead to identifying specific knowledge about which creatures inhabit the desert, and what features or adaptations allow them to survive in this unique desert environment. The active reading net could then be set to sift out how these physical adaptations work, and specifically how they benefit the plant or animal. At the end of the chapter the active reader would then review the 'contents' of their reading net to see

4 WAYS TO BECOME AN ACTIVE READER

1 **Identify the overview.** Before you start to read, take a few minutes to look over the chapter or pages concerned. You are looking for the overview: what is the text about? What clues can you find? The introductory paragraph is likely to introduce what will be learnt, and the concluding paragraph will offer a summary; so, read these first. Typically, each paragraph will make a point and provide evidence to support it with the first or last line of the paragraph making the key point. There may be headings, or sub-headings which will give you a good idea; there might be illustrations or graphs that could help too. This overview helps your mind begin the process of starting to make sense of this potential new knowledge.

2 **Set yourself questions (your 'learning net').** Posing yourself questions before you start reading is the most essential feature of active reading. You could simply be looking for the main idea in the text, or you could be looking for particular examples to support an idea. At this stage of their education, your child is most likely to be looking for facts, evidence or examples to support an answer. Or perhaps they may be trying to understand a point that has previously been confusing.

3 **Now read actively!** This means reading with the intention of finding the answers to the questions you have set.

4 Check understanding. Can you explain the knowledge and examples you have got from the text? Very soon the habits of checking a text for an overview, posing 'learning net' questions to answer as they read, and revisiting understanding, will become invaluable learning habits for your child.

what information had been gleaned about the target topic.

Using active reading skills to analyse and evaluate longer texts

As your child progresses through school they will be given more and more reading material to process. Active reading is a technique that will help them to analyse and evaluate content efficiently and effectively.

The benefits of active reading will enable your child to get far more from their reading, and actually read faster too. Like all skills, active reading improves with practice. Here are four tips to help your child become a strong active reader. ∎

ROGER WEBER/THINKSTOCK

SHIRONOSOV/THINKSTOCK

CRITICAL THINKING PRACTICE

Aged 5–7 years
What are we looking for?

Even at this early stage your child should begin to learn active reading skills. Encouraging your child to be observant about the world around them is a great first step.

• Key Stage 1 reading skills focus on extracting keywords and meanings. This will help them to focus on keywords and draw together clues about important pieces of information.

• Help your child get used to setting their 'learning net' to find out the 5Ws (who, what, why, where and when).

• When your child looks at a story book about say, Jack and the Beanstalk, get them used to actively looking to find information about Jack. Sometimes they will need to double-check information to ensure they have understood, perhaps by comparing a word to a picture.

• Similarly, in a Key Stage 1 reading task ask your child to show you the keywords about a topic. What information can they find about the topic?

• Encourage them to notice any words they don't know the meaning of and see whether they can work these out based on other information on the page. (Afterwards show your child how to look up any unknown words in the dictionary.)

information. When answering reading or comprehension questions:

- Read the question carefully. Pick out and underline the keywords in the question.

- Get an overview of a passage: what is it about? Title and sub-headings will give clues.

- Find the 5Ws: who, what, where, when and why.

- Use keywords from the question in an answer.

- Which facts answer the question best?

- Try to maintain 'active' reading throughout the passage.

Aged 11–13 years
Communicating ideas and information means making sense of the world around you

Practising active reading skills:

- Look up train times on a train timetable.
- Use a dictionary.
- Look up the weather forecast and plan what to wear.
- Look it up: research facts and evidence.
- Find out what is happening in the world: read newspapers.
- Work out best value in the supermarket: compare prices.
- Read or write film or book reviews.

Aged 7–11 years
Using active reading for school work

Active reading can help your child to maximise their marks at school. To apply active reading skills your child should think about what they are looking for from a book or passage before they begin reading. The longer a passage, or the more words on the page, the more your child needs to be clear about what they are looking for.

Your child should set their 'reading net' to search for the most relevant

JON FEINGERSH/THINKSTOCK

TIPS FOR PARENTS

Working out what something means can be just as hard for adults if key pieces of information are missing. Seeing you take time and care to find out what you need to know will help your child learn that developing understanding takes effort and resourcefulness.

• If you don't know what a household symbol means—look it up.

•Make a point of letting your child see you use a map, recipe or instruction guide so that they understand that learning meaning is a lifelong quest.

•Discuss pictures, films or music with your children. Let them see you looking at these from different angles, weighing up what is important to you and what you like and don't like.

• Introduce your children to different sources of information to check facts or get information—for example, how to book a train journey, find a weather forecast, look up book or TV reviews or check news sources that you trust.

Active reading is a mindset. It requires your child to decide what they want to know before they start reading. This could be key words, an overview, or particular facts or other pieces of information.

When you read with a young child you probably intuitively create an active reading mindset by the emphasis you place on keywords and the questions you ask. When your child starts reading by themselves they need to learn to create this active mindset for themselves. You can help them do so by encouraging them to take actions to find and retrieve information.

• If you need some some quick facts—say, from a cookbook, TV guide, or a train timetable—ask your child to find them for you.
• If you are researching a day out, or even a holiday, ask your child to do some research too. What information can they find out about the town from a guide book, or the hotel that you are thinking of staying in? Give your child a research brief of the specifics you are looking for.

Strange but true…

When doing their homework, many children only consult a textbook to look up facts if their teacher has specifically told them to do so. Encourage your child to be independent and resourceful in their research habits and get used to looking for information to support a piece of work of their own accord.

With so many searches for information taking place on the Internet some children would rather google a fact then consult the textbook sitting in their school bag. The same probably applies to you. Don't let consulting a book, and its index, become a lost art! ■

KATARZYNA BIALASIEWICZ/THINKSTOCK

REASONS AND EVIDENCE

ARGUMENT: the framework of reasons and evidence used to support an overall conclusion.

REASONING: the process of using reasons to persuade.

REASON: a statement to support an argument.

CONCLUSION: the statement or belief that the arguer wants to be accepted.

BEING REASONABLE: using reasons to make an argument.

BEING UNREASONABLE: demanding an outcome (or conclusion) with either no reasons, or reasons that do not support the conclusion.

Reasons are the building blocks of logic, and children need to understand and use reasons at every stage of their education, and in the world beyond. Reasoning—or using reasons—is how we make sense of the world around us. It is also the medium of persuasion.

Many parents instinctively use reasons to support guidance or instructions to their children. If you want your child to go to bed on time, you might give them the reason: 'because you were up late last night.' The very presence of the reason helps make the instruction to go to bed become sensible and fair—in other words, reasonable.

Learning to use reasoning is an invaluable life skill. Being able to reason forms a key part of learning to live and work happily and collaboratively with other people. This is because reasons play a pivotal role in helping us either accept or reject ideas, beliefs and actions in a constructive way.

Most crucially, reasoning is the process through which we can test out our ideas and intended actions and quite literally work out which make sense. In addition, effective reasoning is the way to persuade others to accept our point of view. The earlier children work this out, the more likely they are to be able to persuade those around them.

Reason: *'As I have done all of my homework...'*

Conclusion: *'...I should be able to play now.'*

Using reasons helps us to organise our thoughts and decide what to think. Being able to reason is the bedrock of ▶

academic study in every subject throughout your child's school career. For example, in English at Key Stages 1 and 2 there is a significant emphasis on being able to organise ideas. Beyond this stage, as work becomes more challenging, your child will need to structure their work. Being able to use reasons will have a tremendously powerful impact on your child's ability to do this.

To become an active critical thinker your child will need to develop the habit of looking for reasons and deciding whether they are strong or weak. As your child grows up it will become increasingly important for them to learn to think for themselves and evaluate whether an action or belief makes sense.

Looking for reasons and constructing your own takes effort. It is usually so much easier just to react and say the first thing that comes into your head. However, this won't enable your child to consider the whole picture. Keep showing your child that a slower response—when one takes time to plan and consider all aspects of a question—will produce far better results.

'But my child is too young to reason with…'

It is true that in the early years your child's thought processes will be dominated by emotion, but eventually—and this depends on their own rate of maturation—they will be ready to start experimenting with the skills of reasoning. ∎

'When my son was nine years old he asked for a Swiss Army Knife for his birthday. I used reasons to make clear why I was saying no: knives are sharp; I didn't think they were safe for him; I thought he was too young to have and play with tools like this—especially unsupervised. When I said no, he told me that I was being mean, and that was the end of that.

Two years later my son still wanted the Swiss Army Knife but now he knew that he would have to reason with and persuade me if I was to accept the conclusion he wanted (ie that he should be given a Swiss Army Knife).

This was the argument he put forward:

Reason 1: "You want me to spend more time playing outside and making things; if I had a Swiss Army Knife I could use it to play in the garden to carve and shape wood."

Reason 2: "I understand (empathy and reasoning at work together) that you worry that I might cut myself, but I promise not to use the biggest blade, and I will only use the knife for carving wood. If there are other tools on the knife you think I shouldn't use then I promise I won't use these."

Conclusion: "Therefore, I think I am responsible enough to have a Swiss Army Knife for my birthday."

I was persuaded and he got the knife (albeit one without many sharp tools). My son realised that if he wanted me to accept his point of view then he needed to reason with me and respond to my reasons. This involved him empathising with my concerns, reflecting on what he thought were my strongest reasons against him having the knife, and thinking of his own reasons to counter my points.'

MOTHER OF TWO

Sight words
live out people
who work

4. time
5. white
6. bike
7. dime
8. hide
9. ice
10. kite

CRITICAL THINKING
PRACTICE

Help your child recognise and start to use basic reasoning

Affirm and encourage 'being reasonable'. Wherever possible try to use reasons yourself so that your child can hear and learn to recognise reasoning in action.

At this stage the focus should be on introducing the idea of using reasons orally. Encourage your child to recognise a reason when they hear one, and praise their efforts to try to use a reason when they can.

When you ask your child to do something, or tell them that they can't do something, ask them what they think your reasons are.

Encourage your child to follow current affairs. Ask your child to read some of the stories in the news and see if they can identify the reasons given to support a particular point of view.

Ask your child to tell you their reasons for wanting to persuade you of something. Explain to your child that if they want to change your mind about something they are far more likely to do so if they give you reasons. ▶

Aged 5–7 years: Help your child recognise and start to use basic reasoning

Explore patterns as a means of understanding what happens next.

1. Plant some seeds or bulbs. What happens if some have more sun or water?

2. Talk about nature and how the world works; why can't we always see the stars? Why do we have clouds? Why does the moon seem to change shape?

3. Play marbles: what makes them move fast or slow?

4. What makes things change? Explore the impact of hot and cold. Make and then melt an ice cube. Melt some chocolate.

5. Ask questions about films and books. Which characters are good or bad? Why do the characters behave the way they do?

6. Find connections between ideas and concepts:
   • Play simple card games.
   • Play noughts and crosses.

7. Use knowledge to help make decisions: talk about healthy foods in the supermarket and ask your child to make their own healthy choices.

Aged 7–11 years: Keep encouraging thinking time

Listening, paying attention to, and then working out reasoning all takes time. Encourage your child to slow down and take the time necessary to identify reasons.

1. Learn to build a hypothesis based on clues. Go on a nature walk and try to identify a bird or animal by its footprints. How big is it likely to be? What does a feather tell you? What might it look like?

2. Grow something from seed. How much light, warmth and water does it need? What conditions help the plant grow best?

3. Encourage your child to read or follow a news story every day. Discuss these stories with them.

4. Ask questions about books and films. What makes a character good or bad?

5. Make connections and predict probability:
   - Play card games.
   - Play chess.
   - Play strategy games like Monopoly.

6. Learn to understand the reasoning that supports actions and ideas. Find three reasons in favour of 'I will do my homework now' and three in favour of 'I will do my homework later'. Or, 'All dogs and cats should be microchipped'.

7. Talk about some inventions that human beings depend on, for example, jet engines or the Internet or penicillin. Discuss the pros and cons of each.

8. Identify goals or targets to do with a hobby and then form a plan of action to help achieve them.

9. Use knowledge to plan choices: make a healthy packed lunch.

FORSTER FOREST/THINKSTOCK

INGRAM PUBLISHING/THINKSTOCK

Aged 11–13 years: Ask your child to start thinking about their strongest reason to support a particular idea or point of view

1. Encourage your children to follow current affairs and find reasons in support of both sides of a debate. For example, should Britain build more nuclear power stations?

2. Try discussing the following debate topics with your child and ask them to put forward three reasons for and three reasons against the following statements, and then decide what they think:

   • Smoking should be banned in public places.

   • Circuses shouldn't be allowed to make animals perform in public.

   • Children should be allowed to take time off in term time.

3. Make decisions based on a list of pros and cons, for example, how to spend pocket money, or how to save money.

4. Discuss films and books. What actions or events might have changed the behaviour of key characters?

5. Play chess.

6. Consider an action—say, walking the dog, or going to a museum—and suggest three reasons in support of it.

7. Ask your child to pretend they are Prime Minister—what three problems would they try to solve and how?

8. Identify goals or targets for the next term and specific actions to help achieve them.

9. Use knowledge to make choices: plan a healthy meal and explain the benefits of your choice.

EVIDENCE

Learning how to identify and evaluate evidence is crucial to becoming a strong critical thinker; evidence helps determine the strengths and weaknesses of different claims, as well as what may, or may not, be true. Understanding how to evaluate evidence provides an invaluable life skill, one that your child will need at every stage of their school career and beyond.

Evidence is a body of facts or information that can be used either to support a point being made or to show whether something might be true. At school, evidence is likely to mean facts used in support of a point or statement. Failure to provide evidence could lose a candidate up to a third of all marks in written examinations such as English, history and geography. The good news is that acquiring the habit of providing evidence to support an answer is a sure way for your child to improve their performance.

In the world beyond school it is also very important that your child learns to question claims and opinions and to find out if these are backed up by trustworthy evidence. Even now advertisers will be trying to persuade your children to buy something by making claims about their products. As your child grows up they will be lobbied by politicians, companies, the media, charities and many other bodies. Being able to evaluate the evidence put forward will help your child decide how to react to such lobbying.

As a parent there is a great deal you can do to help your child recognise the many different forms that evidence might take and then evaluate them. First and foremost you can encourage young children's natural curiosity—asking 'why?' or 'how?' is, after all, a search for deeper understanding. ▶

> **Supporting an answer with evidence or an example will almost invariably gain your child extra marks in an exam or essay.**

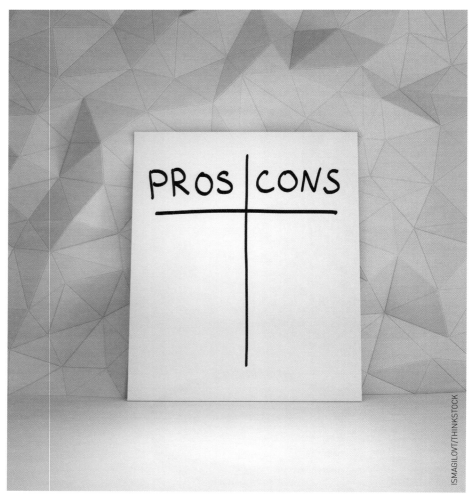
ISMAGILOVT/THINKSTOCK

3 TIPS TO HELP YOUR CHILD EVALUATE EVIDENCE

1 Ask your child to decide if the evidence is strong or weak:
• Is the evidence from an expert?
• What can your child tell you about the sample size in a survey? Is the sample large enough?

2 If evidence is based on what has happened in the past, encourage your child to ask questions like 'has anything changed this year?'

3 When your child expresses an opinion, ask them to provide some evidence to back it up, or suggest that they do some research to find some. (And if they can't find any evidence, perhaps that opinion might need to be reconsidered!)

Older children can use independent research skills to find or test various sources of evidence.

A good way to start is by helping them understand the difference between facts and opinions. There is a very big difference between these two statements: 'I think that spinach is good for you' (which is an opinion with no evidence), and 'Spinach is good for you; my science teacher told me that spinach contains a lot of nutrients to keep us healthy' (which includes evidence from an expert source).

You can help your child to identify and then evaluate others' opinions by asking them to respond to a news story and then assess the evidence supporting their own point of view. For example, you could choose a story such as 'Some wildlife experts think it's wrong to keep pet cats because they are killing all the garden birds'. If your child is fond of cats they might disagree, but what sort of evidence could they use to support their view?

Types of evidence

There are several different types of evidence, and learning to distinguish between them, and to attach the appropriate importance to them, is an important step in becoming a critical

> **Introduce your child to the idea that experts can provide us with evidence to guide us. Talk to your child about the advice that they receive from experts—such as doctors, nurses or teachers.**

> **A survey can provide very strong evidence if it is large enough to be truly representative. The questions also need to be put to the right people—those who actually know about, or are affected by, a particular issue.**

WAVEBREAKMEDIA LTD/THINKSTOCK

thinker. For example, an **eyewitness account** of an event can provide credible evidence, more so than someone who is reporting second-hand, but only so long as the witness can be regarded as a neutral observer.

Sometimes evidence is put forward on the basis of an individual's **personal viewpoint or bias.** If that individual is obviously representative of, or sympathetic to a group, then this could affect the value of the evidence. For example, 'My 13-year-old and her friends went to see One Direction and thought they were amazing!' has a different force to 'My granny saw One Direction and hated them!'

An **expert** is often the source of reliable evidence. Take the statement: 'The vet said our dog is getting too fat and we need to stop feeding him titbits'. The vet's expert opinion provides far more weight than 'My brother says dogs should eat whatever they want to'.

Surveys can be presented as evidence for people's opinion, so it is very important to determine whether the information they offer was collected by an impartial source, is relevant to the issue, and is sufficient in terms of sample size. A survey conducted by an expert authority—for example, a medical trial carried out by a university science department with a large sample over a number of years—is likely to provide strong evidence. On the other hand, a survey carried out with a small number of individuals of the wrong age group, sex, and/or economic background may offer weak evidence.

Evidence—or speculation?
Sometimes 'evidence' is put forward in predictions about the future. For example, in the debates surrounding most general elections each side puts forward so called 'evidence' to support their claims that their party will provide the best Government. However, usually such 'evidence', however credible its source, is in fact simply speculation. ■

Beware of little words that can have a big impact on interpreting statistics:

'Sale: Up to 50% off!'

'Up to' can be very misleading; all this means is that the discount will not exceed 50%—the vast majority of the discounts might only be 5% or 10%.

Over half of people think that... sounds as if it means the great majority. In fact it could just mean 50.01%.

Average. The word 'average' is often used very carelessly. What does an 'average' girl or 'average' boy actually mean?

CRITICAL THINKING
PRACTICE

Aged 5–7 years
Weighing and measuring

• Test the claim: A carton of orange juice is enough for a glass of orange juice every day for a whole week. How many glasses of orange juice are there in a carton? What size would the glass need to be?

• Or: A bottle of bubble bath can last for two weeks. How many good bubble baths can you get out of a bottle of bubble bath?

• Do sunflowers grow better in a sunny place? Try growing a sunflower from seed in a pot; get your child to move the plant from sunny to shady spots and see what happens.

• 'Our family's favourite breakfast cereal is cornflakes.' Get your child to ask each family member what their favourite cereal is and see whether the results of this mini-study support the claim.

Aged 7–11 years
Spot the evidence

• Introduce your child to some trustworthy sources of evidence: a textbook or encyclopaedia, or perhaps a reliable news website for world current affairs.

• When your child reads, listens or watches a news story ask them what evidence they have noticed? Was it an individual expert, a survey or some form of statistics?

• Encourage your child to look more closely at the claims made by advertisers—can they find any evidence to support these?

• Ask your child to look at the information on food packaging. Does this provide evidence of healthy or unhealthy food content?

Aged 11-13 years
Gathering and evaluating evidence

In 2015 *First News*, a children's newspaper, conducted a national survey on 'The State of Britain's Children' amongst 2000 children in the UK aged 7–14 years old. This study looked at how happy children felt and how they felt about the future. Look at this survey (P48-49) with your child and see if they can answer the questions below.

1. Is the survey relevant to the issue being considered?

2. How big is the sample size?

3. Does the sample represent the relevant groups?

4. Who paid for the research? Do they have anything to gain?

5. How was the information gathered? (For example, a survey on a busy city street may not be the best environment for people to speak openly about their personal opinions.)

6. Do you think the survey offers useful evidence?

In 2015, First News, one of the leading newspapers for children, embarked on a mission to find out the state of Britain's children: Are they happy? How do they feel about the future? What's really happening in their schools and in their home lives? More than 2,000 children, aged between 7 and 14, across the UK took part.

THE STATE OF BRITAIN'S CHILDREN — KEY FINDINGS
EMOTIONAL WELLBEING

THE STATE OF BRITAIN'S CHILDREN — KEY FINDINGS
SCHOOL

More than **80%** of children believe they have a good or very good life compared with other children in Britain. Children from the North East think they have it best.

Almost a third of children say they don't get enough peace and quiet.

Crime and terrorism is the second biggest fear after worries about families and way above concerns about issues such as the environment.

75% of children are happy or very happy at school and a huge **95%** are happy or very happy at home!

Concerned about giving your child an email address? Don't be—**97%** of children say they have never been bullied via email.

76% of 14 year olds have never been bullied online. Face-to-face bullying is a bigger problem—**46%** say they have been bullied face to face, compared to **12%** on a social media platform.

Nearly **50%** of children surveyed say they feel lost when they don't have access to a phone, tablet or computer. 25% of children said that not having access to a phone, tablet or computer makes them feel left out.

More than 50% of children surveyed aren't sure that what they are taught at school will help them in later life. This opinion becomes more prevalent as children get older. At seven years old, **88%** of children think that what they are taught at school will help them as an adult. However, by 14 years old, only **36%** think so.

Schools may wish to bolster their pastoral care at the end of primary school and in the first year of secondary school. Our survey shows that **children are most worried in years 6 and 7.** Encompassing everything from happiness and health right through to money and popularity, our survey shows that 10 and 11 year olds are more stressed out than any other age group—affecting a huge **79%** of ten year olds and **76%** of seven year olds.

A third of all children are already worrying about getting a job when they finish school. But it's London's kids who are the most concerned... When asked if they are worried about getting a job when they leave school over **43%** said yes. Very much focussing on the 'now', over **37%** of kids in the South West aren't even thinking about getting a job after school.

THE STATE OF BRITAIN'S CHILDREN — KEY FINDINGS
PARENTS

SUPER MUM
YOU'RE NUMBER ONE!

A whopping **70%** of children aged 7-14 cite their mum as the person who understands them best. However, as children get older, there is a gradual shift—whereby children start to think that their friends understand them better. At the age of seven, only one in 50 children think their friends understand them best but, by 14 years old, this has soared to one in every ten.

7.7%

1 in 10

North East dads aren't listening! On average 20% of the children surveyed say it's their dad who understands them best. This statistic is fairly equal regionally. However a huge exception is revealed in the North East, where only 7.7% of children selected their dad.

THE STATE OF BRITAIN'S CHILDREN — KEY FINDINGS
PHYSICAL APPEARANCE

Kids' confidence in their appearance seems to dwindle as they get older. While over **40%** of 7 year olds say they think they are pretty/handsome, by the age of 13 this figure has fallen to a self-conscious **18%**.

Less than half of kids think about what they post online being seen by people in the future.

Boys are more brand-conscious than girls and think it's more important to wear the 'coolest' clothing. They are also more concerned about having the same mobile phone as their friends. By contrast, more than **55%** of girls say they don't agree that clothing brands or the make of their mobile is that important.

London kids are the most appearance conscious with over 95% of them thinking about their looks. By contrast, **14% of Welsh children don't even think about how they look**. Londoners also think they're the best looking, whereas **children in the East of England rate their looks the least**.

Predictably the style and brand of clothes becomes a far more important consideration for children as they get older. In fact, the importance of having the 'right' clothes doubles between the ages of 7 and 14.

63% of girls surveyed admit to taking at least one selfie every single day! More than a third of girls take up to five selfies a day. And regionally, the Welsh take more selfies than anyone else.

PARENTS
DO IT YOURSELF

The best way to help your child develop reasoning skills is to be a great reasoning role model. Hearing you use reasons to support your point of view is the best way to help your child 'tune in' to reasoning.

Let your child see you consider both sides of an argument

If your child is to learn good reasoning habits from you it is important they see you consider both sides of an argument. Make it clear that you are prepared to hear and think about both points of view. Explain to your child which reason finally persuaded you to support one side or the other.

Be prepared to change your mind

Being prepared to change your mind is a clear indication that you are genuinely open-minded and prepared to reconsider something if the reason is strong enough. Work out the pros and cons and then decide. Consider reasons and evidence for and against a possible action before you decide.

- Kitchen debates: take a topic that members of your family don't agree on and look at the arguments for and against.

Discuss current affairs

Discuss news stories from the radio and television—every news bulletin contains news items with conflicting points of view. Explain which reasons you find persuasive and why.

Check out the evidence yourself

Just as with other aspects of critical thinking, your child is far more likely to learn to identify and evaluate evidence if they see you using evidence to guide your opinions and help make decisions.

- Make your child aware that you pay attention to evidence.
- Explain what evidence you find most helpful and why—personal recommendations (from first hand witnesses), experts, expert sources (books or specialist websites), media sources or surveys.
- Make it clear when you feel you can't give an opinion without finding out more evidence.
- Talk to your children about news stories and explain how a piece of evidence has had an impact on your views. For example, with the Syrian refugee crisis public opinion changed considerably when people realised the devastating consequences of the risks refugees were taking to flee from conflict.
- Point out to your child when you feel there is *no*

evidence, and when you spot a controversial media headline that is not substantiated by any hard facts.

- Talk to your child about the presentation of 'health' or 'lifestyle' surveys (these crop up virtually weekly) and how regularly they contradict each other.
- Talk to your children about food labelling and how it helps you decide what to buy.
- Going for a day out or on holiday: how have first-hand accounts helped you decide where to and where not to go to?
- For big purchases—say, a new car—explain what research you are doing and how you compare and contrast the evidence about the benefits of different cars.
- Looking after the environment: what evidence has helped you decide whether you recycle, turn off light switches, or use less fuel?
- Staying healthy—what evidence helps you decide how best to stay healthy?

Assuming your kitchen is the hub of the family home, make it the hub of evidence checking too. Keep some reference books on a kitchen shelf that you and the whole family can use. ∎

- Quality or quantity: identify pros and cons in support of using your weekly household food budget to buy either better quality or a greater quantity.
- Reflect on 'big budget' buying decisions: research pros and cons.
- Question buying choices: is your decision to buy branded items based on experience and facts or advertising hype?

GOLDEN RULES

Using principles or golden rules to organise and guide thinking and decision making makes sense. The hallmark of a principle or a Golden Rule is that it provides a generally accepted truth or guidance that can be widely applied to many different situations.

As so many beliefs and actions are dictated by principles it is very important that children learn to recognise them and their impact on reasoning.

Most children are introduced to some non-negotiable rules—or principles of behaviour—very early on. These are likely to be rules or guidelines that parents regard as profoundly important—like staying safe, or not being rude or unkind. As children get older they will become aware of more principles like being fair, respecting equality, following the rule of law, and respecting other cultures and faiths. In the home environment, a Golden Rule might be something considered non-negotiable—like always trying to be kind or telling the truth.

Using principles

Principles are extremely helpful to critical thinkers. Including a principle when you are trying to persuade someone invariably makes reasoning stronger.

'*I think you should invite Jack to the party; he is a new boy and it would be great for him to have a chance to make friends.*'

Principle: '*It would be the kind thing to do*'.

> **A Golden Rule is a moral maxim or principle found in many cultures and religions and is related to fundamental human nature—such as, 'Treat others as you would like to be treated'.**

'Divide the cake up so that everyone gets a piece.'

Principle: *'It is important to be fair'.*

Spotting how the influence of a principle shapes reasoning also makes it far easier to understand someone else's point of view. When a child understands that a parent's reasoning is likely to be dominated by principles such as staying safe or being polite, the parent's reasons and actions make far more sense.

Helping your child understand how principles work provides a positive framework for parenting. If you make the basis of your reasoning clear it will usually make far more sense to your child than simply saying 'No—that's wrong'. For example, *'Don't kick the dog. You know you should always be kind to animals'.*

Be clear and consistent about your Golden Rules and how these shape your expectations of your child. Try to help your child make sense of the world by explaining the principles that might be guiding other people's actions. People don't always agree or believe the same things, but understanding other people's principles will help your child to learn to respect opinions other than their own.

Young children are still learning how to behave and what constitutes right and wrong. However, even by the age of four most children will have some pretty good ground rules in place. The more a child understands what is expected of them, the more they can make sense of the world around them.

Understanding these guidelines creates a framework for both behaviour and reasoning: 'You know I expect you to be kind to everyone, so …' or *'You know it is wrong to tell fibs, so …'* This understanding will help your child learn and understand better what is considered either reasonable or unreasonable behaviour.

Introduce the idea of Golden Rules that are your non-negotiables, like staying safe, being kind and telling the truth. Helping your child understand how Golden Rules—and later principles—relate to expectations of behaviour will help your child make sense of reasoning.

As your child becomes a teenager, conflict will not be far away. Managing this conflict by being aware of, and respecting each other's principles will help achieve some calmer solutions. Many parent/teenage conflicts revolve around the parent's natural desire to keep their child safe v the teenager's equally natural desire to become more independent. Respecting both of these points of view will help both sides compromise.

Developing an understanding of the impact of principles on our own reasoning and in the wider world is an essential part of becoming a strong critical thinker. This understanding will be tremendously powerful in helping your child express their own beliefs, as well as understand the reasoning forming the basis of the beliefs of others.

As you follow current affairs at home, encourage your child to consider the principles behind an action and ask them if they agree. For example, when governments block refugees from war-torn countries they are preserving their resources to look after their own communities. But do we all have a responsibility to look after people outside of our own countries? Or, should companies be prevented from putting potentially harmful amounts of sugar in food or should we be allowed to eat anything we like?

Principles

Discuss with your child how principles have a positive impact on the world around them. Ask them what these principles mean to them. If they support these principles, what actions might follow?

▶

NATALIELEB/THINKSTOCK

For example:

Principle: Everyone is as important as you are.

Action: 'So, I clear up after myself at lunch and don't leave it for the dinner lady'.

Principles to discuss over breakfast:

- Treat other people the way that you would like to be treated yourself.
- Be kind to others.
- Always try to eat healthy food.
- You should always tell the truth.
- We should be kind to animals.
- Be safe on the Internet.
- Everyone deserves a chance.
- It is everyone's responsibility to look after the planet.

Discuss with your child which principles are most important to them.

Can they link any of their actions or beliefs to these principles?

Debate

As your child becomes more mature they will be increasingly more sophisticated in their ability to see how principles shape the world we live in.

Understanding principles will help your child develop their own beliefs and decide what issues are important to them. They will also begin to understand that principles are not always absolutes—for example, are there ever times when it is okay not to tell the truth? Or, how can you preserve the resources of the planet when so many people live on the poverty line?

Some principles seem to clash:

- Farmers should be allowed to farm in a way that destroys an animal's habitat.
  Principles: No-one should be hungry v we should protect animals.

- The Government should raise taxes to allow the NHS to provide the best treatment for every patient.
  Principles: We should look after one another v we should have freedom of choice over how to spend our own money.

- Everyone should be free to say what they like, even if it incites people to terrorist actions.
  Principles: Freedom of speech v you should not cause harm to others. ∎

MONKEY BUSINESS IMAGES LTD/THINKSTOCK

TIPS FOR PARENTS

Which principles do you hold most dear in your family? Are there any Golden Rules that you would consider fundamental to the way you behave at home, and expect others to behave?

Discuss some of the issues raised in this chapter with your child and encourage them to think of reasons to support both points of view. Then decide which side of the argument you support.

Helping your child to develop their skills of debating is a crucial step on the path to becoming a true critical thinker. Allow your child to see you arguing in a way that is non-aggressive, putting your side of an argument in a firm but reasoned way.

How well do you listen when you are arguing with your child or other family members? Lead by example when it comes to seeing both sides of every argument. ■

HOW CAN YOU IDENTIFY 'FAKE NEWS'?

CREDIBILITY

ONEINCHPUNCH/THINKSTOCK

Knowing who to believe can be tricky for both children and adults. Every day the media, retailers, governments, politicians and a host of other interest groups lobby to try to persuade us to believe what they have to say.

Critical thinking techniques can provide your child with a quick checklist to help them work out who is the most believable, and which sources of information are likely to be the most reliable and credible.

Every day your child will need to work out what they should or should not believe when they read a newspaper or watch TV. Or perhaps what evidence to accept about a range of issues: which is the best laptop or mobile phone to buy or what makes a healthy diet.

Social media is also full of claims and so-called 'evidence', and the sheer speed and volume of e-messaging means that it has, arguably, never been more important to be able to assess the credibility of an individual source and decide whether a claim or a piece of evidence is believable.

The RAVEN technique

The RAVEN technique gives pupils a checklist of questions to ask about a source of information. Sources will come in all shapes and sizes: a source could be an individual person, an organisation, a newspaper, a website, or perhaps a school book. Asking RAVEN questions enables children to decide how believable they think a source or piece of evidence might be.

'RAVEN' is a skill that can be applied to virtually any source or piece of evidence and is applied by taking time to ask yourself a series of questions about the source. Pausing to apply the RAVEN technique will help give your child the ability to think and judge what to believe for themselves, and not be tempted to simply believe everything they hear or read.

    R = Reputation
    A = Ability to see (are there
          any first-hand witnesses?)
    V = Vested interest
    E = Expertise
    N = Neutrality

Young children obviously won't be mature enough to understand and ask all of the RAVEN questions but parents can help encourage children to start asking some questions about what they see or hear. Asking RAVEN questions—in language appropriate for the age of your child—will help.

Reputation

What kind of reputation does the source of information have?

Past behaviour is often used to help make a judgement about an issue in the present. For example, a CV builds a picture of an individual's past career history, and references give us an idea of whether that individual has a reputation for being a hard worker, or an honest person. Past behaviour is certainly no guarantee that an individual will behave similarly in the future, but it is reasonable to let a past positive reputation be an influencing factor. So, when your child is considering how believable an individual's statement or piece of evidence is, it can be helpful to consider the reputation of that individual.

Organisations also have reputations.

For example, the BBC has a reputation for reporting the news accurately and fairly. If you hear or see a story from the BBC its reputation for honest news reporting is likely to strengthen the 'believability' or credibility of the story.

Conversely, after the financial crisis the reputation of the banking industry became extremely negative with the whole sector being categorised as greedy, reckless and dishonest. Arguably the subsequent actions of both governments and regulators were influenced by this reputation.

PHOTOMARU/THINKSTOCK

A negative reputation does not mean that the whole sector will behave in this way in the future (or indeed behaved in this way in the past). However,

> The power for stories to 'go viral' means that there is a great possibility for claims to come to be believed on the basis of numbers of 'likes' or 'views' rather than because there is clear evidence of first-hand testimony. 'Likes' or 'views' are a bit like hearsay evidence which is based on second-hand information that has been passed down the line from the person who originally saw or heard it.

the shadow of this reputation has influenced our view of the credibility of a bank's claims that it has its customers' interests at heart.

Ability to see

Ability to see refers to what an individual can 'see' or perceive with any of their five senses.

A claim, or piece of evidence, is usually strengthened if it can be supported by an eye-witness, someone who can back up a point because of their first-hand sensory experience.

The first-hand eye-witness account of someone who actually saw, heard, touched or tasted an experience or event is more persuasive than someone who has not been informed by any of these sensory experiences. So, a battle scene described by a soldier or a reporter in a combat zone is far more believable than an account from someone hundreds of miles away from the front line. Or someone describing which phone you should buy is far

more believable if they have actually used it themselves.

Having a strong 'ability to see' usually strengthens the credibility of an individual and is an important factor to keep in mind when deciding on the credibility of a story.

Vested interest

Where an individual or organisation has something to lose or gain, they are said to have a vested interest. So, although their claims may be absolutely true, you have to keep in mind that what they have to say may be influenced by what they have to lose or gain by saying it. Having a vested interest can either strengthen or weaken credibility.

For example, the BBC has a vested interest to protect its reputation for accurate news reporting because it does not want to lose its reputation for high quality reporting. The desire not to lose its reputation is likely to mean that it will be motivated to work hard to continue to report the news accurately; its vested interest to protect its reputation will therefore strengthen its credibility.

On the other hand, a tabloid newspaper that depends on high circulation to sell advertising will want to print headlines that sell newspapers. If circulation goes down, advertising revenue will fall; so, this vested interest to protect profit may encourage the use of salacious headlines that help sell the newspaper, but are not always as accurate as they might be.

Advertisers obviously have a vested interest to sell their product. So, when a skin care company makes claims about its product, you have to keep in mind that their desire to make money means they have a vested interest only to tell you what is good about their product.

So, when considering how trustworthy a claim or piece of evidence is, it is important to encourage your child to think about issues of vested interest. Who has something to lose or gain? Could this be influencing their claim or evidence?

Expertise

A claim that is backed up by an expert witness is considered more believable than one that is not. Again, encourage your child to listen to the news and notice how many times 'experts' are consulted, or asked to give their opinions. However, it is important that the expert has expertise or experience that is relevant to the issue.

Neutrality

The last credibility criterion of RAVEN is neutrality: not supporting either side and having no reason to favour one side or the other. An individual who is neutral will have no reason—or motivation—to lie, or distort the truth. Someone who is truly neutral can be expected to represent both sides of a dispute fairly. Therefore, a neutral witness is likely to be more credible than one who is biased one way or the other. ∎

REAL EXAMPLE: 'I'm confident we can get a good deal for Britain in Europe—and we can fix those things that need to be fixed.' – David Cameron, Prime Minister

KAPTNALI/THINKSTOCK

How would you assess David Cameron's tweet about the changes he hoped to obtain in the EU before the Brexit referendum?

Reputation: The PM had a reputation for being a good negotiator and this gave his words credibility.

Ability to see: He was negotiating with other leaders in person, and had a high-level team who were also likely to be dealing with a number of powerful individuals in the EU. So, he and his team were able to see 'first hand' how successful they were likely to be with their negotiations. This strengthened their credibility.

Vested interest: However, he had a vested interest to promote his own success; if he was unsuccessful with his negotiations he was likely to lose the support of his MPs, as well as the general voting public in the UK. This weakened his credibility.

Expertise: He was an experienced politician, and had considerable expertise in negotiating in Europe which strengthened his credibility.

Neutrality: He was definitely not neutral. He was trying to protect and promote Britain's rights, but was clearly not looking to promote or represent the opinions of those opposing him.

Conclusion: Although David Cameron's strong reputation, ability to see and expertise all strengthened his credibility, his very obvious and weighty vested interest to try and maintain party and national support made his tweet hard to accept as credible, or believable, on face value.

REAL EXAMPLE: 'As you know I have said, and got a fair amount of flak for it within parts of the Church, we have to accept, and quite rightly, that the Same-Sex Marriage Act is law, and that it's right and proper, it's the law of the land, and that's great.' – Justin Welby, Archbishop of Canterbury, quoted in **The Telegraph**

The Archbishop voted against the Same-Sex Marriage Act in the House of Lords last year.

In his first interview with a gay publication, the Most Rev Justin Welby told Pink News that the Church had to accept that same-sex marriage is now the law in England and Wales.

From Justin Welby's words above, should you believe that he will support same-sex marriage in the Church of England?

Reputation: As leader of the Church of England, the Archbishop has a reputation to maintain the core beliefs of the Church, and there has been much opposition to gay marriage within the Church. The Archbishop voted against the Same-Sex Marriage Act in the House of Lords. Therefore, the Archbishop may have developed a reputation for being anti-gay marriage. This reputation may make his words 'that's great' hard to believe. However, as leader of the Church of England he also has a reputation for keeping and supporting the laws of the land. His professional reputation as a 'keeper of the law' would thus make his words credible.

Ability to see: As leader of the Church of England he has access to, and speaks for, every church in England and Wales. As a member of the House of Lords he also understands how the law works. His first-hand access to both key members of the Church and the structures of law increases his credibility.

Vested interest: The Archbishop has a vested interest to protect his reputation for truth and fairness, and as an upholder of the law of England. He has a strong interest in upholding and promoting the decisions of Parliament (even if he voted against them in the House of Lords). This vested interest greatly strengthens the believability, or credibility, of his statement.

However, the Archbishop has a difficult path to follow. He also has a vested interest in the unity of his Church. This vested interest suggests that he may not wish to offer support to gay marriage within the Church of England. However, he has chosen his words carefully, and made it clear that it is the duty of the Church to support the laws of England and that this is 'right and proper'. By emphasising the duty to keep the law, he has made it clear that this is his primary interest. Again, this strengthens his credibility.

Expertise: The Archbishop can be expected to have great expertise in theology and the teachings of the Church and a comprehensive understanding of the daily inner workings of the Church; as a member of the House of Lords he also has a strong understanding of the law. We can therefore see that he has more than enough expertise for his statement, 'We have to accept the Same-Sex Marriage Act is law' to be believable.

Neutrality: By voting against the Same-Sex Marriage Act in the House of Lords it is clear that he is not neutral about the issue of gay marriage. On the face of it, this would weaken his credibility.

Conclusion: Although it is clear that the Archbishop is not neutral on this subject, his strong vested interest to protect the integrity of both Parliament and the Church, and his undoubted status as an expert in this field, considerably strengthens the credibility of his words.

CRITICAL THINKING
PRACTICE

Aged 5–7 years
Who should your children believe?

At this age, although children will be too young to understand how to apply the RAVEN technique, they are old enough for you to start setting the scene.

Start introducing your child to the **'A' and 'E' of RAVEN: ability to see and expertise.**

1. Encourage your child to start asking 'How do they know?' questions.

Ability to see: explain that first-hand witnesses—people who saw or heard it for themselves—are likely to be more believable than people who weren't there.

On nature walks, encourage your child to think about what they can learn for themselves from what they can see, hear, or touch.

Show your child what they can learn from touch. Give your child a number of different textures to touch. Or perhaps, something cold—like an ice cube—and something warm. Talk about how much more they learn about these substances by experiencing them for themselves.

Cookery (again!)—what does your child learn by tasting food, rather than being told what it tastes like?

2. Point out the experts.

Help your child understand that information provided by expert individuals is more believable because they are experts in the field. Talk to your child about the experts that you both know and the kind of expert advice they could offer. For example:

Specialist shop assistant: *expert knowledge of products offered*

Train guard at a station: *expert knowledge of train times/destinations*

Doctor or nurse: *expert knowledge of illnesses and how to stay healthy*

Teacher: *expert subject knowledge*

Vet: *expert knowledge about looking after animals*

However, you also need to make it clear to your child that you have to ask the *right* expert. The train guard won't know about animals, and the vet won't know about trains!

▶

Aged 7–11 years
Who should your child believe?

By now your child is likely to be developing some 'consumer awareness' and will be beginning to develop their own consumer likes and dislikes. These might relate to games or technology, books, comics, TV or films, meals out or maybe even cars or holiday destinations.

When your child is considering which products they would like to buy, encourage them to learn more from different sources to find out which product might suit them best. Again, concentrating on the 'A' and 'E' of RAVEN, ask them if friends who have 'first-hand' knowledge of the products would recommend them or if they can find any experts who can provide some reliable advice.

Looks can be deceiving

Look through some magazines or holiday brochures with your child and look at the pictures. Discuss some of the pictures and images of products and destinations. Ask your child if products they buy typically look the same as pictures in adverts. Are there any instances when your child has been disappointed that a product didn't look the same? Was there any way that they could have found other information to see what the product might really have been like?

Look at some pictures of ready meals on food packaging—does it look that way in real life?

Discuss with your child why advertisers try to make pictures and images so appealing.

Aged 11–13 years
Now try asking all of the RAVEN questions

Your child is old enough to try and assess how reliable a source might be by asking all of the RAVEN questions.

Red Bull, the energy drink company, had to pay more than $13m (£8m) to settle a class action lawsuit for misleading consumers with promises of increased physical and mental performance.

Some adverts can be very misleading—

encourage your child to ask questions about the claims that advertisers make about their products. Can they find any claims by advertisers that they don't agree with?

Introduce your child to the **'R' of RAVEN—Reputation.** Encourage your child to consider the reputations of the products and services they are interested in. What kind of reputation do companies like Nike, Apple or the BBC have?

Some tabloid newspapers have a reputation for exaggeration or mis-representing the facts; being mindful of this kind of reputation can be a useful reminder to look a little more deeply into a story before accepting a potentially misleading headline.

Now consider the **'V' of RAVEN—Vested Interest.** When an individual or organisation has something to lose or gain, they may be tempted only to talk about the advantages of a product or situation. Encourage your child to look and listen to some adverts and notice that you virtually never hear anything negative about the product. This one sided view usually makes the advert less believable.

Finally, look at the **'N' of RAVEN—Neutrality.** Encourage your child to try to find a neutral source whenever they can.

With all of the RAVEN questions in mind, watch the news with your child and ask them to ask questions when they hear or see two conflicting sides of a story put forward. Which side offers the best eye-witness accounts from the most neutral sources, or the most expert input? Which side has the better reputation? Does either side have a vested interest (something to lose or gain)? Weighing up all of this information will help your child work out for themselves which side is more believable. ∎

DIGITAL VISION/THINKSTOCK

TIPS FOR PARENTS

Reading newspapers or watching the news

Try asking RAVEN questions yourself when you read or watch the news. Share with your child which aspects of RAVEN help you make up your mind and which sources you feel you can rely on. Are you more persuaded by expert opinion or first-hand experience? And how alert are you to vested interest?

Help your child work out which news sources they can rely on

Many parents and teachers encourage students to read newspapers. However, students are just as frequently warned that they shouldn't believe everything they see and hear in the media. Assessing the credibility of sources is a basic critical thinking skill, and one that can help your child make their own sound evaluation of what they read and see.

When your child watches the news, or reads a newspaper, encourage them to notice how many eye witness accounts they can spot. Discuss with them the difference such an account makes to the view they form of the story. Conversely if your child declares a fact or claim to be true, suggest that they check to see if this view is supported by any first-hand accounts.

RAVEN can help with day-to-day issues too

Sometimes your child may be influenced by friends who are trying to persuade them to do something that neither they nor their friends have any real knowledge of. Encourage your child to ask enough questions so that they can make up their own mind based on a real understanding of the issue.

Use RAVEN to evaluate the credibility of websites

The Internet is a huge place with an enormous amount of information. Encourage your child to use RAVEN to try to evaluate which websites genuinely provide credible information. ∎

CLUE WORDS

THE BASIC LANGUAGE OF REASONING

If you have young children, it's likely that you are already using basic reasoning language to communicate ideas of 'why', 'how' and 'what'.

'WHY' = reasons. Most parents will provide their children with reasons to support an action or instruction.

'HOW' = examples or evidence. These back up reasons.

'WHAT' = conclusions. The conclusion is usually the thing you want your child to do or accept (or, indeed, that your child may want you to accept!).

INSTRUCTION: 'Don't touch the plate!'

REASON: 'Your plate is very hot and may scald you'.

EXAMPLE: 'Remember when your cousin touched the plate and burnt her finger?'

CONCLUSION: 'So, don't touch the plate!'

Reasoning is the process of thinking about something in a logical way and using reasons and evidence to support or reject a belief or action. Learning to reason involves being aware of the presence or absence of reasoning.

However simple or complex a question, the process of reasoning doesn't really change. The most important aspect is finding a way to identify what information you do or don't have and then working out how you can best evaluate it.

While a very young child will certainly not be capable of sophisticated reasoning, the good news is that there are a number of words, quite commonly used, that help flag or identify the presence of reasoning. As they become familiar with these your child will start to recognise reasons, evidence and conclusions. Getting into the habit of using these 'clue' or 'indicator' words will also help your child begin to structure their own reasoning.

Get clued up on 'indicator' words

The ability to organise thoughts into structured reasoning is a tremendous strength that will be a powerful boost to your child's learning at every stage of their education. One of the best ways to help your child understand the reasoning process is to use 'clue' or 'indicator' words that flag the presence of reasoning. These words signpost to the reader or listener where they are in the reasoning process and what type ▶

BESTGREENSCREEN/THINKSTOCK

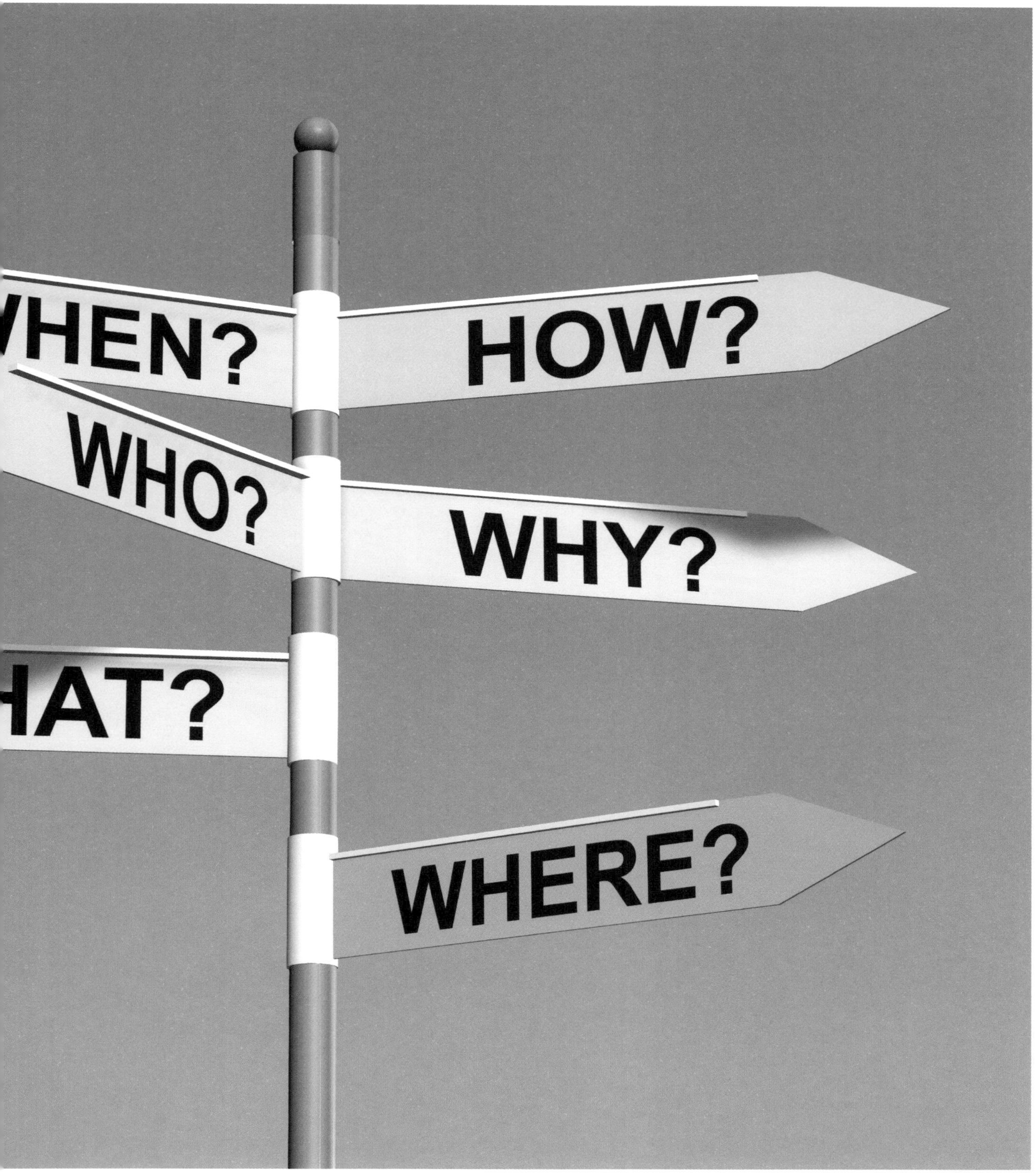
HOW?
WHO?
WHY?
WHERE?

KEY INDICATOR WORDS

REASONING INDICATORS

These are the words that link an action or idea to a consequence or conclusion.

Reasoning indicators include words like **because, as, since.**

Reasoning: 'Because you stayed up late last night you are now very tired'.

EVIDENCE INDICATORS

Strong reasoning makes use of examples and evidence to strengthen the forthcoming conclusion.

Example and evidence indicators are words like, **for example, such as, for instance.**

Reasoning, plus evidence: 'Because you stayed up late last night you were too tired to do nice things such as go on a bike ride'.

CONCLUSION INDICATORS

A conclusion is the 'outcome' of reasoning. Getting your child used to hearing the indicator words that announce conclusions (the action that you want them to accept) will help them notice the most important part of a message, even if the rest of the words before or after are sometimes lost on them. Similarly, teaching your child to use indicator words will help them sort out for themselves what they regard as the most important part of their own message. Conclusion indicators are words like **therefore** and **so.**

Reasoning, plus evidence, plus conclusion: 'Because you stayed up late last night you were too tired to do nice things such as go on a bike ride, **so** you **should** go to bed early tonight'.

It is helpful for your child to recognise words and phrases that indicate that a conclusion is coming: **must, should, need, ought.** If you can present what might otherwise be taken simply as a bossy order, as actually the conclusion of your reasoning, backed up where necessary by evidence or examples, you are much more likely to get your child to do what you want them to do. And the same applies to your child. If they can try to persuade you or others to do what they want, by using reasoning, evidence and conclusions, they will feel much more in control of their lives and consequently be much happier.

of reasoning they can expect to see or hear next.

Recognising reasoning indicator words will not only enable young children to understand and learn more, it will also help them organise their thoughts and begin to learn how to present their ideas in a logical and persuasive way. One of the great things about getting into the habit of using indicator words is that the words themselves act as a reminder to include that aspect of reasoning. For example, using the word 'because' reminds you to include a reason. Using 'for example' reminds you to give examples to support your reasons. The ability to present ideas clearly supported by reasons, evidence and a conclusion is a 'must have' skill throughout your child's school career and beyond. ∎

CRITICAL THINKING PRACTICE

NICK_THOMPSON/THINKSTOCK

Aged 5–7 years

The goal in these years is for your child to become familiar with basic reasoning indicator words and to recognise that 'because' usually means there is a reason coming, or that 'must' or 'should' usually flag an order or instruction. Encourage your child to use simple indicator words themselves as a means of organising their thoughts and ideas. If indicator words are missing from your child's language, insert them to prompt your child to think further: 'You want to go into the garden *because*…?' Or, 'You don't like rice pudding, *so*…?'

Aged 7–11 years

As your child gets older he or she should be able to use basic reasoning indicator words quite comfortably. Help expand their reasoning vocabulary by using or pointing out less obvious reasoning cues. These could include evidence indicators: **for example, such as, for instance**, or conclusions: **therefore, must, should, so.** At this age your child may also start to employ '**empathy**' indicators to enhance complex or persuasive arguments. ▶

AMIT VASHISHT/THINKSTOCK

Aged 11–13 years

From 11–13 years, your child will be expected to start organising their ideas and arguments in an increasingly structured way. If your child has acquired the habit of using reasoning indicator words it should lead to higher marks at school because written work in all subjects will require reasons to back up a point and evidence to support reasons. You may not be as closely involved with your child's academic work at this stage but you can:

• Encourage your child always to use a reason indicator word in their written work (because/since/as), as using one of these words will remind them to include a reason.

• Try offering them a reason indicator word as a prompt if they are struggling to think of a reason to back up a point. Simply offering up the word 'because' will often help them kick-start their thinking.

Eg 'King Henry VIII divorced Katherine of Aragon because ...'

• Encourage your child to get into the habit of spotting reasons by listening or watching out for reasoning indicator words.

• Prompt your child to watch out for other points of view. Strong critical thinkers need to be able to keep an open mind and look at an issue from more than one standpoint. Words and

phrases like 'on the other hand', 'some suggest', or 'alternatively' indicate the presence of another point of view.

• When your child is trying to persuade you about something ask them to 'tell you their reason'.

• Encourage them to use indicator words themselves.

• If your child is struggling to formulate a reason, try introducing an indicator word as a prompt to help. Simply offering your child a prompt will do a great deal to help them begin to formulate a reason.

Eg '**Because** I have tidied up...'
'**As** I have eaten all of my supper...'

MY SON'S SWISS ARMY KNIFE ARGUMENT

(see page 38) with indicator words added

Reason and example: '**BECAUSE** you want me to spend more time outside, I could use the Swiss Army Knife to do things in the garden, **SUCH AS** carving wood'.

Empathy: '**ALTHOUGH** I understand you worry I might cut myself, I promise not to use the biggest blade, and I will only use the knife to carve wood. If there are other tools on the knife you think I shouldn't use, then I promise I won't use those either'.

Conclusion: '**THEREFORE**, I think I am old enough to have a Swiss Army knife for my birthday'.

WAVEBREAKMEDIA LTD/THINKSTOCK

TIPS FOR PARENTS

Try to include clue words whenever you can.

By regularly using clue or indicator words you can help your child recognise the presence and function of reasoning. Using words that flag the presence of a reason, a conclusion, an example or piece of evidence will help your child become aware of the various component parts that make up a reasoned argument.

Clue or indicator words can be used in both simple and complex reasoning (in fact they work even better with complex reasoning). This is because hearing a clue word will help your child work out what is coming next. When you say 'because...' your child will recognise that a reason is about to follow. Similarly, the word 'therefore...' is likely to signal that a conclusion is about to follow. Meanwhile words 'such as' or 'for instance' will alert your child to the presence of examples that are being used in support of reasons.

Other clue words indicate the presence of a counter argument, or alternative point of view such as 'on the other hand' or 'alternatively...'

Remember, your child first has to be aware of the presence of reasoning before they can learn to evaluate it. Using clue words is a great way of helping your child recognise reasoning for themselves. ■

FLAWED ARGUMENTS

A flawed argument is a lapse in logic, or a fracture or weakness in reasoning. When there is a flaw in an argument, reasoned thinking has not been applied. This may have happened by accident because an issue seems too difficult to think through, or deliberately because sometimes it is easier to put down the views of others by 'cheating the reasoning process' and using a flawed argument instead.

Your child will become a stronger critical thinker if they can learn both how to spot flaws in the arguments of others in the wider world around them, as well as avoid lapsing into flawed arguments themselves in either their own written or spoken answers. Like all critical thinking, learning to avoid flawed arguments means thinking actively, and learning to avoid trying to take 'thinking short-cuts'.

Flawed arguments will cause reasoning to become faulty. The degree to which the presence of the flaw damages reasoning will depend on what other strands of reasoning are present to support it. Sometimes something just sounds or looks wrong. Identifying a flawed argument enables you to be able to pinpoint the weakness it causes with accuracy and work out exactly what might be going wrong with an argument.

There are several types of flawed arguments to be aware of:

Circular argument

As the name suggests, a circular argument is one that goes around and around and never moves forward in a reasoned way. This is because the reason and the conclusion are both basically saying the same thing.

Reason: 'Because my new iPhone is really great...'
Conclusion: 'Therefore it is the best'.

Or

Reason: 'I find that subject dull...'
Conclusion: 'Therefore it's really boring'.

In both cases the conclusion and the reason are more or less saying the same thing, instead of offering a distinct reason that offers strong support to its conclusion. Younger children have a tendency to lapse into circular arguments and need to be encouraged to think their way out of them. Offering them some

GOIR/THINKSTOCK

prompt words like 'why' and then a reason indicator word like 'because' can help move their thinking forward (rather than it going around and around).

Restricting the options

The flaw of 'restricting the options' is when two choices are presented as the only possible way forward, when in fact a variety of other options are available and possible. This type of argument tends to be created when the arguer actively wants to push you into a particular course of action (even when other options are possible). So, the arguer presents one option that is clearly very unappealing beside the course of action they want you to take.

You and your child will not have to look very hard to find examples of 'restricting the options' in the wider world. All of the following headlines would be guilty of this flaw:

'Close Britain's borders to immigrants

or face housing chaos.'

'Create more speed humps or accept more will die on Britain's roads.'

'Raise interest rates or let pensioners' incomes wither.'

All of these statements have been sensationally presented, and are offered in a 'restricting the options' format—asking us either to accept the first point or suffer the consequences of the second.

Ad hominem (the name-calling argument)

An ad hominem argument (also known as 'attacking the arguer') is when an opposing view is dismissed by attacking the person putting the view forward instead of considering and responding to the view itself. This might be in the form of name calling, or generally attacking something about the person. Quite often someone might decide to 'attack the arguer' when they don't want to address the argument itself, and ▶

HIGHWAYSTARZ-PHOTOGRAPHY/THINKSTOCK

saying something abusive is seen as an easier way to disagree.

'*Victoria Beckham says … How can we accept the view of a former Spice Girl?*'

It may be that Victoria Beckham's view is both informed and persuasive, but in this sentence the arguer dismisses her views, simply on the basis that she was a former Spice Girl.

'*What can David Cameron possibly know about this issue? After all, he is an Old Etonian!*'

Similarly, in this example, David Cameron is being attacked because he went to Eton, and his views dismissed simply because of this.

Closer to home, your child can probably offer their own examples of 'attacking the arguer' where perhaps someone at school has called someone names rather than listen and consider their views.

Ad hominem flawed arguments can also come about because of prejudice against individuals or groups, particularly in a cultural context. Again, work with your child to help them realise that views are being dismissed because of prejudice rather than because there is a reasonable case for rejecting the opinion.

Generalisations

A *hasty* generalisation takes an insufficient piece of evidence and uses it to generalise, to establish a general conclusion.

A sweeping generalisation is a flaw that creates stereotypes. So, for example, '*Some bankers behaved badly in the financial crash. Therefore, all bankers behave badly. He is a banker, and so you can expect him to behave badly too.*'

Conflation

The flaw of conflation treats two separate concepts as one and the same. For example, in Nazi Germany, Hitler conflated Germany's economic problems with 'the Jewish problem'. Similarly, in the media today, you will see some stories 'conflate' the issues of immigration with economic problems, or even crime, when clearly these should be considered as separate issues. The very significant danger of conflation is that it is likely to result in an issue or problem being attributed to the wrong cause.

Reasoning from wrong actions

Two wrongs don't make a right. Arguing in defence of a wrong action simply because this wrong behaviour is already being done by another person, company or even country does not justify the wrong action.

For example, some states defend their own ill-treatment of suspects in custody on the basis that the US allegedly ill-treated detainees at Guantanamo, America's controversial prison camp in Cuba. Many countries accused of breaches of human rights actively try to defend their actions by citing similar actions in other parts of the world. Such an argument would commit the flaw of reasoning from wrong actions.

Causal flaws

Quite often there might be a correlation between events, but it would be a flawed argument to suggest that simply because two things happen at the same time, one causes the other. For example, shark attacks and ice cream sales both rise in the summer months, but one does not cause the other. ∎

GOIR/THINKSTOCK

AUTHOR'S TIPS

3 WAYS TO TEACH YOUR CHILD ABOUT FLAWS

Adults often deliberately deploy the flaw of 'restricting the options' to persuade their children into a course of action. The flaw works by only offering two courses of action, one of which will be very unappealing, when there were actually many other possibilities available. eg 'If you don't do your homework tonight you will fail your exams!'

1 Encourage your child to watch out for this flaw in news stories in newspapers, on radio or TV. It will not be hard to find examples, particularly in the tabloid press.

2 Ask your child to watch out for this flaw with people they know (including you!) and explain how and why they feel the flaw has been committed. It can be quite rewarding for your child to outwit an adult!

3 When your child identifies an example of 'restricting the options', ask them to think about what other options were really available.

CRITICAL THINKING
PRACTICE

Aged 5–7 years
Developing habits that will help your child avoid flaws

Very young children may be too young to understand the logic of flaws but they are old enough to start developing good thinking habits to avoid slipping into flaws of their own.

Help your child get out of a circular argument rut

In a circular argument the reason and the conclusion are basically the same thing. Young children often slip into circular arguments because they haven't yet worked out how to identify the reason that might support an action.

If you hear your child getting stuck in a circular argument rut, where the reason and the conclusion are virtually saying the same thing, try to jog them out of it. Ask them to give you a reason that focuses on a different idea, but still supports their conclusion. Sometimes asking your child 'Why?' and offering the prompt of the indicator word 'because' will help move the argument forward to include a persuasive reason. *'Why do you think History is a boring subject? Is it because...'*

Developing the mindset to help avoid falling into other flaws
Reasoning from wrong actions
Most children (and many adults!) will try to justify a wrong action on the basis that someone else has done it. They will need you to explain that other people doing something wrong does not make their wrong action right.

Think about the last week. Can your child think of any wrong actions that they tried to justify because other people had done them?

Causal flaw
We constantly struggle to understand what causes things. A causal flaw results when we identify the wrong cause of an outcome. Getting your child to consider causes will help them develop the mindset to be open-minded.

• The plant has withered. What might have caused this? Too little water? Or not enough sun?

• Your cornflakes have gone soggy. Why do you think this is?

• Why do you think your team won the match today?

Aged 7–11 years
Learning to avoid the bad habits of flaws...

Developing strong critical thinking habits means being aware of flawed arguments and how they can lead to poor reasoning. Your child will still need indicator word prompts such as 'because' to avoid them slipping into circular arguments. Similarly, they are also likely to need picking up when they try to justify a wrong action on the basis that other people are doing it.

Encourage your child to keep an open mind and be prepared to question and reconsider their own thinking. To help this process, ask them what would make them change their mind about something.

Causal flaws

Your child will be old enough to consider possible causes for a wide range of issues. Explain that there are often many different causes behind a problem or issue and that identifying the correct cause is often very difficult.

Discuss with your child some of the big debates of our time—like possible causes of global warming. Or perhaps—controversially—child obesity. Do they think that some children are overweight because of too much sugar, too much junk food, not enough exercise or possibly all of these things? Do they think that a 'sugar tax' on fizzy drinks would help remedy the situation?

Attacking the arguer (ad hominem)
Help your child avoid prejudice
In the flaw of 'attacking the arguer' reasons are ignored and something about the arguer is attacked instead. It is often easier to attack those who seem different from us in some way. If you hear them 'attacking the arguer' rather than focusing on that person's reasons, point this out to your child. Explore with your child their reasons for doing so, and explain that everyone's views should be considered on their own merits, and one should not make judgements about people because of the way they look or sound.

Aged 11–13 years
Encourage your child to watch out for flaws

By now your child should be able to identify flaws like circular arguments, attacking the arguer and some causal flaws. Encourage them to be observant and point these out to you when they see and hear them. Doing so will help them understand more about weaknesses in reasoning. ■

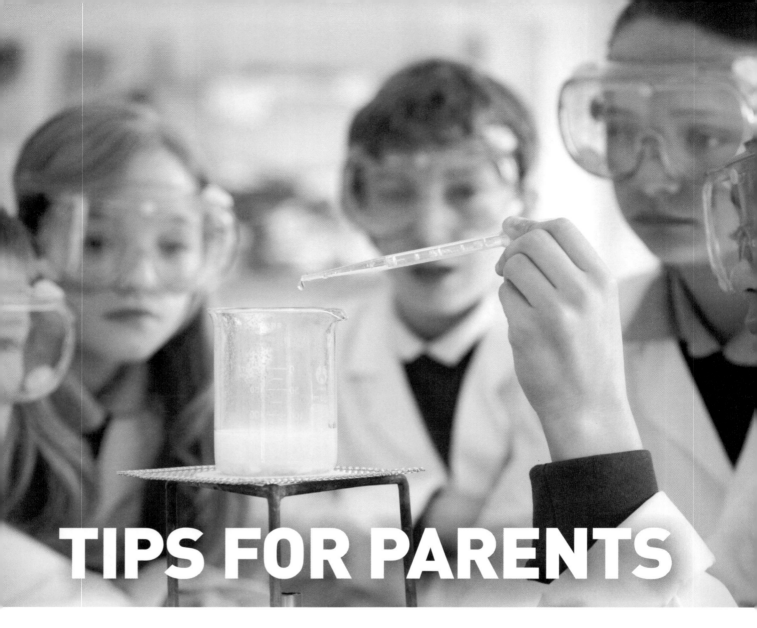

TIPS FOR PARENTS

Learning to identify and avoid flawed arguments requires some strong critical thinking habits. Some people refer to these habits as critical thinking virtues: courage, curiosity and independence.

Encourage your child to develop the CT virtues of courage, curiosity and independence

Being prepared to question reasoning takes **courage**. It can be very hard to question the reasoning of other people, particularly if theirs is the majority view.

Curiosity is needed if your child is to consider other possible explanations or ways of thinking.

Independence is also a must if your child is to learn to be guided by their own thinking rather than that of other people.

Are you guilty of flawed reasoning?

Watch out for your own flawed reasoning. Being prepared to share your 'flawed moments' with your child will help improve their understanding of flaws.

Circular arguments:
- Attacking the arguer
- Reasoning from wrong actions
- Restricting the options
- Causal flaws
- Generalisation

Similarly, when you hear or see a 'flaw in action' explain these to your child. If you watch the news or look through a popular daily newspaper together it won't take you very long to find one. ∎

APPEALS

An appeal to emotion is a persuasive device that uses emotion to try to persuade you to accept a point that is being made, sometimes in place of compelling evidence.

An appeal to emotion

Many views are formed, and decisions made, on the basis of emotion. There is often nothing wrong with this. However, it is important to realise when emotion is playing a role in your opinion or decision-making process.

An appeal to emotion works to win support by appealing to emotions rather than offering reasons. This type of appeal might be appealing to any one of a very wide range of emotions— guilt, sympathy, pride, vanity, anger, patriotism—all of these powerful emotions can be appealed to play a role in influencing opinions and decision making.

Making an emotional decision is not necessarily a bad thing, but it is important that your child knows when they are letting their 'heart rule their head', or, at least when they are giving their emotions a big vote in the decision-making process. It is also wise to know when those around them— either at school or in the wider world— are using emotion to try to win their support.

It is especially important to understand when emotions are being manipulated to try to win support for extremist views, and history is littered with examples.

Hitler's use of emotional appeals

Hitler's oratory was packed with emotional language. When Hitler ▶

called for the German people 'to resist the yoke of Jews and Communists', he appealed to (and arguably created) the emotion of 'national fear' as his words suggested that Jews and Communists had the ability to enslave the German people. Similarly, when Hitler called to the German people to create a new empire which would rule the world for 1,000 years, he created and appealed to the emotion of national pride.

In much the same way, in his wartime speeches, Winston Churchill made emotional appeals to the emotions of loyalty, pride and patriotism:

'… We shall prove ourselves once again able to defend our Island home, to ride out the storm of war, and to outlive the tyranny, if necessary for years, if necessary alone….. That is the will of Parliament and the nation.' (Winston Churchill, 4th June 1940).

Advertising and emotional appeals

Many advertisements are based on emotional appeals.

Appeals to sympathy

Consider advertisements by charities trying to move us to make donations. Such adverts often feature pictures of starving children or images of animals in distress. These emotional appeals do not mean that the charity does not have a valid case for support. However, if a charity uses these type of images it is important to realise that such images are appealing to emotions of sympathy, pity, guilt or even anger as part of their case to win support.

MACIBLINK/THINKSTOCK

MOODBOARD/THINKSTOCK

Appeals to vanity

Consider images used by cosmetic companies, or the fashion industry. There will be many photographs chosen because they play on the emotion of vanity, or a desire to 'look cool'.

Peer pressure

Peer pressure can be a powerful influence. Quite often your child might feel peer pressure because they believe that 'everybody is doing…' or 'everybody thinks…'. The pressures to conform to what everyone else is doing can be overwhelming for many young people, and recognising these pressures for what they are is the sign of an accomplished critical thinker.

E-popularity

Think about Facebook's 'likes' or 'trending', or the colossal number of views on YouTube. Knowing that hundreds or thousands, or

even millions of people have 'liked' or 'viewed' an article can be very persuasive in encouraging support for an issue, irrespective of the merits of the issue or story being followed.

Of course it is possible that the issue or story may be extremely important

'Sending a kid out onto the Internet these days without teaching them critical thinking skills is like asking them to go to bat at home plate with a giant goldfish. The results are squishy, the kids have the chance of taking damage, and worse—they can't hit the ball out of the intellectual park.'
Betsy Akoki, Microsoft

and should receive widespread attention and support. However, it is also possible that a story or issue might 'go viral' simply because of the very human tendency to follow the crowd. An appeal to e-popularity feeds off this tendency.

The power and scale of social media means that it is really important to teach your child to recognise an appeal to e-popularity ('trending' or 'number of views' or 'likes'), to evaluate the appeal and to ask if they are reading the story/following the issue simply because of the number of people who are doing the same. Are they being influenced by the sheer number of 'views'?

It may be that a popular e-story has merit; perhaps it is an important issue that deserves national or international support. However, it is important that your child retains their own active thinking and works to decide the merits of the issue themselves. ∎

CRITICAL THINKING PRACTICE

Child aged 5–7 years
Becoming aware of emotional appeals

Your child won't yet be able to understand the implications of being persuaded to think something because of the way they feel. However, you can begin to help raise your child's awareness of the impact of some advertising images.

Discuss these images with your child and ask them how they make them feel.

GULAY SAKALLI/THINKSTOCK

Child aged 7–11 years
Understanding how emotions can motivate actions

By now your child will be able to understand more about how and when they act on their emotions. Discuss these images with your child. Do any of these pictures make your child want to support the causes or charities they represent? Discuss why.

GULAY SAKALLI/THINKSTOCK

HERMERA/GETTY IMAGES/THINKSTOCK

Child aged 11–13 years
How might emotional appeals be impacting on your child?

Study these images with your child and discuss with them what messages they send out.
How might one protect oneself from the pressures involved in these types of images?

AIMING HIGH

OMGIMAGES/THINKSTOCK

The habits and techniques of critical thinking will benefit your child in their day-to-day learning. They can also help them make the most of their own thinking power to maximise marks in tests and senior school entrance exams. In short, critical thinking techniques allow your child to aim high.

'Critical thinking is the sort of thinking that takes conscious effort and involves reshaping knowledge, not simply the recall of facts... It is the kind of thinking that demands initiative.'

Dr Mike Dash, Chief Research & Development Officer, MACAT

Critical thinking habits for the exam room

Taking time to think

Aged 11+ or 13+ your child should be absolutely clear that their best response to a question or problem comes after thinking has taken place. An instant response to an exam question is unlikely to be as strong as a well thought out answer.

▶

ABLE IMAGES/THINKSTOCK

> Learning to use the language of reasoning will help your child improve their writing skills in English.
>
> Pupils should be encouraged to consider what they are going to write before beginning by:
>
> • planning or saying out loud what they are going to write about
>
> • writing down ideas and/ or keywords, including new vocabulary
>
> • encapsulating what they want to say, sentence by sentence
>
> • identifying how language, structure, and presentation contribute to meaning
>
> Extract from Department for Education National Curriculum English programme of study for Key Stages 1 & 2

By now, phrases like 'think before you answer' should be taken literally by your child. An instant response means that your child will not have had time to think through the implications of a question. Thinking time gives your child the chance to consider what they need to know in order to answer the question.

Use active reading skills to notice detail

Small details often have a disproportionate impact on meaning. Missing an important detail in the exam room—much as facts, names, numbers, or an instruction in a question—is likely to lose your child valuable marks. Not reading the question properly is a remarkably common mistake made by exam candidates. Therefore, noticing and retrieving detail is a very important critical thinking skill to master.

From a purely exam perspective it is imperative that your child gets into the habit of taking note of detail. All exams contain important details that must be acted on to achieve top marks, and as the exams get harder the important details that need noting can become harder to spot.

Clarify meaning

It is important to encourage your child into the habit of double-checking and querying meaning; if they have misunderstood the question they will not be able to answer it correctly. Communicating ideas and actions is not always an easy business; often words, phrases, symbols or pictures can be interpreted in many different ways and there is ample opportunity for misunderstandings to occur. A key critical thinking skill is to clarify meaning and double-check what is meant. Similarly, it is very important

evaluate reasons is a very important skill throughout your child's school and higher education career, and is an invaluable skill for use in the wider world.

Principles can be used as 'super reasons' as they are based on widely accepted truths. Reasons are needed to support beliefs and actions; in critical thinking language, reasons support conclusions (the belief or action that we are being asked to accept) and form the body of an argument. A persuasive reason has the potential to shape beliefs or actions, or perhaps even change opinions.

Using indicator words

Indicator words help flag or signpost the function that the surrounding words are performing. For example, words like, 'therefore, so, thus, must, should' flag that a conclusion (the point of the argument) is about to follow. Or, words like, 'because, as, since' indicate the presence of a reason.

There are two benefits to your child using indicator words. Firstly, it makes meaning clearer to whoever is listening to or reading what is being said or written. Secondly—and perhaps even more importantly—using the appropriate indicator word provides a framework that tips our brain into actually providing the conclusion, or giving a reason (both needed to maximise marks in a test situation).

Evidence and examples

Every answer should strive to include evidence and examples to support a reason.

Conclusion

A conclusion is the final point or answer. In a time-pressured exam situation sometimes a student can forget to include this! ■

for your child to try to communicate their ideas and points with care, and as accurately as possible.

Use reasoning elements to organise ideas and structure answers

In an exam or test situation your child will be required to analyse exactly what the question is asking and work out what aspects of their knowledge can offer the best response. Reasoning elements—such as principles, reasons, indicator words, evidence and examples—provide a framework through which your child can organise their ideas and structure answers.

Often a child will write a lot of words for an answer but fail either to include keywords, a reason, evidence or an example. For example, why is something so? What is the most important reason? What piece of evidence could support this? Is there a good example?

Using reasons

Reasons are an essential reasoning tool and form the bedrock of the reasoning process. Being able to identify and

INTERVIEWS

Even very young children may find themselves in an interview situation in which they are asked to respond to a range of questions and show off their thinking processes. This might be to win a place at a competitive prep school, or perhaps more likely at 11+ or 13+ as part of a senior school entrance or scholarship assessment. Most interviews will be quite low key, and simply be a means of learning more about your child, and how they think. However, scholarship interviews will be far more demanding and designed to assess academic potential and your child's ability and desire to think critically.

Applying basic critical thinking techniques will provide your child with strategies that help them organise their thoughts, demonstrate what they know, show off their thinking skills, and give them the confidence to believe that they know how to do their best in an interview situation.

The benefit of applying critical thinking techniques to an interviewer's questions is that they enable your child to answer any question to the best of their ability. Your child is far better off responding to the questions asked, rather than trying to show off to the interviewer by attempting to regurgitate a lot of memorised material. What will absolutely not impress the interviewer is a series of rehearsed answers that are merely offered up in response to the prompt of a question. Such answers are totally inadequate because they will not show the interviewer how your child thinks, and do not provide any insight into your child's abilities. Worse still, rehearsed statements stick out like a sore thumb, and the interviewer may (correctly!)

AMELIA FOX/THINKSTOCK

deduce that the statements or ideas being offered might not be evidence of your child's own thinking processes.

Your child is far more likely to impress the interviewer with their own, perhaps hesitant, answers pieced together step by step, as a result of their own critical thinking, even if these contain a mistake or two. This will be the genuine product of your child's own thinking processes and their ability to make connections, build an answer, and perhaps even offer some original insight.

Being asked questions by an interviewer in a new and unfamiliar environment can be a daunting experience. This situation is likely to be even more worrying if your child senses that you are anxious too. Try to keep things as low key as possible. Whilst it might be helpful to give your child some general advice, resist the temptation to give your child specific content for an answer. Their best answers will come from using their own thinking skills to respond to the

questions that are actually being asked.

What matters most is the way that your child approaches interview questions, and if they respond to every question using their critical thinking techniques they will be well equipped to give their best possible response to each question. In a way, thinking correctly can be compared to hitting a tennis ball well; if you remember to do a number of small things—keep your eye on the ball, move and put your feet in the right place, hold your racket with the right grip, and follow your swing all the way through—you are far more likely to hit the ball well, and hit well with consistency. The same can be said of the interview; if your child can get used to acting on a series of habits and techniques with *every* question they are far more likely to answer every question to the very best of their ability.

So, keep encouraging your child to: focus on the keywords, think about the question, take enough thinking time, put forward reasons and support them

wherever possible with evidence and examples, and always have a go at a question, even when they don't know the answer. ∎

PREPARING FOR A SCHOLARSHIP INTERVIEW

'In a scholarship interview I want to be able to see how a child's mind is working. Is he or she actually thinking and considering the question I am asking? Are they logical—how do they try to sort out their thoughts? Can they make connections? Do their answers offer evidence of self-awareness? Are they reflective? Is the child an original thinker?'
Scholarship interviewer at a major English boarding school

8 INTERVIEW TIPS
TO SHARE WITH YOUR CHILD

1 Ask for more information if you have not fully understood the question.

2 Respond to the question that is actually being asked. Resist jumping in and talking about the topic rather than the question. Take care to answer the question and not to go off the point.

3 Don't be afraid to make clear what you don't know. If your child is unfamiliar with some of the knowledge needed to answer the question encourage them to explain the gaps in their knowledge, and say that they will answer the question based on what they do know.

4 Take time to think before answering.

5 If a question asks 'Why do you think that...' be sure to give reasons in your answer.

6 Wherever possible support each reason with evidence or examples.

7 If a question asks 'How could something be improved...' or 'Think of another way that you could achieve...', don't be afraid to offer theories.

8 In questions like, 'Why is it important that...' remember that a principle could be used as a 'super reason'.

THE IMPORTANCE OF OFFERING EVIDENCE

Any of your child's answers to interview questions should be supported by well-chosen evidence. The student who can provide evidence in the form of specific evidence and examples that are relevant to the question will be far more persuasive than the student who offers no evidence.

Also, providing well-chosen evidence gives the interviewer the chance to ask supplementary questions that may give your child the opportunity to show off their abilities.

Interview question:
'Do you think you are good at problem solving?'
Answer:
'I like having a go at problems...'
Evidence: 'In science I tried to build an object that could fly/In history I tried to work out who killed the princes in the tower/In maths I have tried some algebra by myself to see if I can work it out'.

JULIEF 514/THINKSTOCK

TIPS
FOR INTERVIEWS

Child aged 5–7 years
Helping your child build interview confidence

Tell your child not to worry about hesitating before they answer; the interviewer will be pleased to see they know how to use thinking time!

Make clear to your child that the interview is to help the school get to know them better. At this stage there are no right or wrong answers. Encourage your child to follow these steps:

• Listen carefully to a question.

• Think about the keywords in the question.

• Don't be afraid to take time to think about the question before answering.

• Try to back up your answer with an example.

• Remind your child that giving an example helps the interviewer get to know them better.

Question: Do you like animals?

Answer: Yes—I love cats. I have a cat called Jaspar, and I like playing with him.

Question: What is your favourite activity at school?

Answer: I like art. I really like painting—last week we did pictures of ourselves which was fun.

MONKEY BUSINESS IMAGES LTD/THINKSTOCK

Child aged 7–11 years
Helping your child show off their thinking skills at interview

- If unsure, always clarify the question.
- Take thinking time.
- Offer evidence and examples if you can.
- Even if you don't know—have a go!

If your child isn't sure what the interviewer means, they should never be afraid of asking for more information, or even what a word means. This shows the interviewer that they're paying attention to key details through active listening—and they will also impress the interviewer with their fact-finding curiosity.

They should always try to support an answer with evidence or an example if they can. Needless to say, the evidence your child offers in an interview situation also needs to be true! Otherwise they will very quickly be caught out by the interviewer if they have not actually read the books or had the experience they are claiming.

For example, an interviewer will not be convinced by the statement 'I love reading' on its own, but they may be very impressed by an answer that details out the books your child read, as well as their thoughts on why they liked or didn't like them. These details offer compelling evidence about your child's love of reading.

INTERVIEW TIPS TO SHARE WITH YOUR CHILD
- Don't be afraid to clarify a question, or ask for more information before answering.
- Take time to think before answering.
- Don't be tempted to give an answer that sounds good (eg 'I love reading the books of Charles Dickens') if it isn't true. You will be caught out!
- Always try to give an example to support an answer.
- If you don't know the answer—take your best guess based on what you do know.

MOODBOARD/THINKSTOCK

Child aged 11–13 years
Helping your child excel at interview

• **Show off your thinking processes.**

• **Don't worry about what you don't know—base your answer on what you know so far.**

By now your child should have acquired the very good habit of not being afraid to ask what a word means or for more information about a question. Taking time to think before speaking should also have become second nature. Quite often there may be no right or wrong answer and the interviewer will simply be trying to learn more about how your child thinks. Encourage them to explain their thought processes as they try to answer the question and offer up evidence or examples to support their reasoning.

TIPS FOR PARENTS

Children are acutely tuned in to their parents' actions and reactions. They will learn an enormous amount from your behaviour. How you respond to their attempts to learn will shape their attitude to learning and intellectual risk taking. They will also pick up on your habits—so it's important that you practise the active habits and techniques of critical thinking yourself.

Be a good critical thinking role model

Let your child see you making use of critical thinking skills in the world around you.

Use reasoning yourself

Don't fall back on saying 'because I told you so'. Instead, use reasons and evidence to persuade your child to do or accept something, and encourage them to recognise what those reasons are.

Principles

Explain the principles that guide your actions.

Think aloud

Thinking aloud as you go about daily chores will help your child learn from your thinking processes. Talk about the problem you are trying to solve, and the possible solutions.

Try not to slip into using flawed arguments

Point out to your child when you see flaws in action—like attacking the arguer or restricting the options.

Try to be open-minded

As a good critical thinking role model, try to let your child see you consider the reasoning and evidence behind conflicting points of view before you make up your own mind.

Help your child be aware of prejudice

Encourage your child to consider the views of others on their own merits.

Don't solve their problems for them

Resist the temptation to do all of the thinking—let your child have a go! Allowing your child to practise their problem-solving skills in the routines of daily life will make them far more confident and competent as critical thinkers.

Help your child become a problem solver

Boost your child's thinking confidence by encouraging them to see themselves as a problem solver.

Manage your reactions

A negative reaction to failure can make a child averse to taking intellectual risks, and this is very difficult to reverse. Be aware that your reactions play a very important part in building your child's confidence to become a critical thinker. Your child must see that a wrong answer will not remove the smile from your face. ■

CLAUDIO VALDES/THINKSTOCK

INDEX

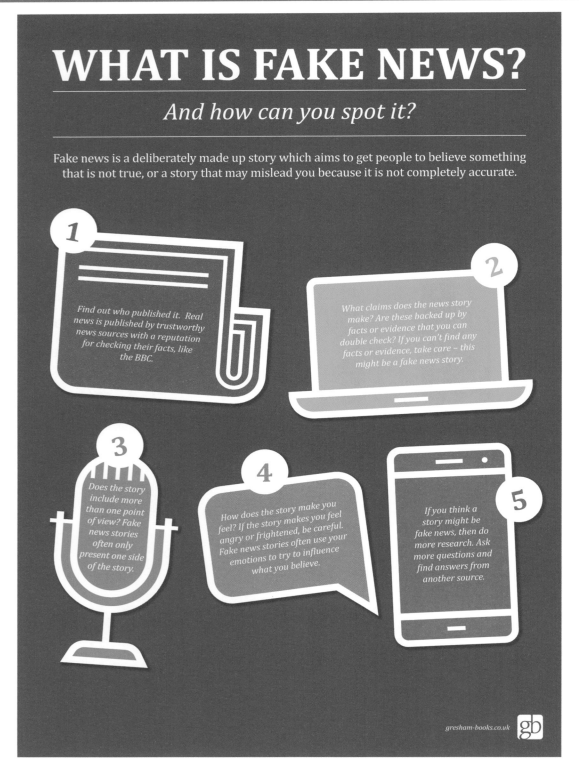

Fake News Poster

Democracy Poster

What is the Rule of Law?

Six rules which help us tell whether the legal system is working correctly or not. Together, these rules form the Rule of Law.

1
Everyone should know what laws they need to obey.

2
Laws should be the same for everyone.

3
We should always use laws, not just our own opinion of what seems right or wrong, to decide if someone has broken the law.

4
Judges, the police and members of the Government must always use their powers fairly.

5
Everyone accused of breaking the law should have a fair trial. They should be treated as 'innocent until proved guilty'.

6
Laws should always try to protect our Human Rights.

If all of these principles are being followed, you can be pretty sure the Rule of Law is working well.

KS2 & KS3 British Values Books

gresham-books.co.uk

Rule of Law Poster

Separation of Powers

The Separation of Powers is a fundamental principle at the heart of our parliamentary democracy.

Legislature
= Parliament
Parliament makes the country's laws.

Executive
= Government
The Government uses laws to run our country.

Judiciary
= the judges
The judges interpret and apply the laws.

Separation of Powers

The Legislature, Executive and Judiciary all have different responsibilities and are separate from one another. Because the Legislature is independent of the Executive, laws can only be altered or introduced with the approval of the Legislature. And because the Judiciary is independent of the Executive, it is free to ensure that laws are interpreted correctly and applied fairly.

The Separation of Powers helps to protect our Human Rights by ensuring the Executive maintains the Rule of Law.

KS2 & KS3 British Values Books

gresham-books.co.uk
gb

Separation of Powers Poster

The British Values Series

An ideal support to help children practise their own critical thinking skills.

Books aimed at Key Stage 2 students

It's the Law!

An introduction to the civil and criminal law of England and how living under the rule of law protects individual citizens.

ISBN 978-0-946095-75-9

Let's Vote On It!

An introduction to democracy and the workings of Parliament and an explanation of how citizens can influence decision making through the democratic process.

ISBN 978-0-946095-78-0

Other titles in the Key Stage 2 British Values series

Our Country, Our World
An explanation of the wide range of cultural traditions to be found in multi-cultural Britain to help students acquire an appreciation of, and respect for, their own and other cultures.

ISBN 978-0-946095-77-3

Looking after Britain
An easy to understand explanation of the public sector and the services provided to British citizens: from the military, police and national infrastructure, to education, health and government.

ISBN 978-0-946095-76-6

Books aimed at Key Stage 3 students

The Rule of Law in Britain
An ideal resource for KS3 students enabling them to distinguish right from wrong and to respect the civil and criminal law, encouraging an appreciation that living under the rule of law protects individual citizens and is essential for their wellbeing and safety.

ISBN 978-0-946095-88-9

The Public Sector in Britain
Written for KS3 students explaining how public institutions and services work and how some public bodies such as the police and the army are accountable to Parliament while others, such as the judiciary, are independent.

ISBN 978-0-946095-90-2

Tolerance and Harmony in Britain
An ideal resource for KS3 students, encouraging students of all cultural traditions to understand that the freedom to choose and hold faiths and beliefs is protected in law, and that it is a fundamental British value to identify and combat discrimination.

ISBN 978-0-946095-89-6

Democracy in Britain
The ideal book for KS3 students encouraging respect for democracy and support for participation in the democratic processes, including respect for the basis on which the law is made and applied in Britain.

ISBN 978-0-946095-87-2

To order books and posters from the British Values series visit **theparentbrief.com/shop/**

Other titles in The Parent Brief series

University Entrance
A parent's guide to UK university entrance and more
Jonathan Watts and Cora Saint

Your son or daughter would like to go to university. How can you help them get in? More than just a 'how to' on Personal Statements and application forms (although we cover that too), this book guides you through the whole process, along with expert advice from teachers, careers advisors, and the universities themselves.

- The indispensable UCAS guide to finding the right university and getting in
- Tips to ace the interview and write a winning Personal Statement
- Packed with practical checklists and real-life tips from parents who have gone through the process themselves

ISBN 978-0-946095-61-2

Wellbeing
The essential guide to my child's physical and mental health
Julie Johnson

Wellbeing is a word found almost everywhere these days but what does it actually mean for your child? This book will guide you through all the challenges of raising a happy and healthy child – physically and emotionally. We've gathered together case studies, expert research, and tips from psychologists to bring you the complete overview.

- Forget the tabloids: here's the truth about how much food, sleep and exercise your child really needs
- The indispensable guide to raising a mindful child in a digital age
- Packed with expert advice and real-life tips from parents
- Bonus advice: how to look after your wellbeing at the same time

ISBN 978-0-94609-563-9

Independent School Entrance
Getting my child into the right school from pre-prep to 6th form
Victoria Barker

You want to send your child to an independent school. Where do you go for the best advice? This accessible guide gives you all the information you need to make an informed choice and support your child through the application process. We've gathered together exert advice, case studies and tips from other parents to give you a complete overview in one easy-to-use handbook.

- How to choose and apply to an independent school
- Beyond league tables and prospectuses, advice on everything from choosing a school to financial aid and acing the interview
- Packed with checklists and real-life tips from parents who have already gone through it

ISBN 978-0-946095-59-9

For more information and free advice visit **theparentbrief.com**